MANY BUT ONE

MANY BUT ONE

The Ecumenics of Charity

Dr. J. H. JACKSON

PRESIDENT,
NATIONAL BAPTIST CONVENTION, U.S.A.

SHEED AND WARD - NEW YORK

To My Wife
Maude

PREFACE

THE AUTHOR of this book approaches this study as one interested in ecumenism and one who appreciates its history, present status, and future possibilities. It is his belief that the world has reached an unprecedented crisis with man's twentieth-century discovery of a power that can destroy western civilization in a few brief moments and perhaps even wipe mankind from the face of the earth. The splitting of the atom paved the way for this tragic threat to the life and future existence of mankind. The only answer to this crisis is a sufficient growth in justice, creative human relations, and goodwill. Man must use the moral and spiritual insights at his disposal to rise above war as the method of settling national and international disagreements just as he has outgrown cannibalism as an accepted way of life. It is the author's position that the Judeo-Christian tradition at its best has the dynamism to achieve the end desired and to save mankind from itself, that it might be dedicated to the work of the Kingdom of God as proclaimed by the prophets of old and by Jesus of Nazareth.

The Christian church has the responsibility of not only saving the souls of men, but of saving men and nations from themselves by bringing them into a fellowship of understanding and love under God. But a church divided against itself and at war within itself cannot achieve these noble ends. The church can best render this required service through a united effort as a world fellowship of believers. The author does not believe that fellowship among believers must be postponed until the day of organic union has come. There is an urgent need for world Christian fellowship right now and it can be achieved without each denomination merging into a super-church. However, if this world Christian fellowship is ever to exist, interest and concern must be developed at the grass roots. The ecumenical message must not be left to scholars, to executives of city, state, and national councils or to leaders of the World Council of Churches; this message must be told by laymen, parish priests, and pastors as well.

At this time, there is sufficient agreement on the basic principles of the Christian religion to form this world Christian fellowship, a fellowship that can generate the spirit of tolerance necessary for a broad understanding and a deep appreciation of traditions other than that in which one is born or nurtured. The moral and spiritual needs of our times demand the answer that the Christian church is best qualified to give.

While there is much to be done in achieving the fellowship needed, the author sees some encouraging signs in the historic development of the World Council of Churches and also in the growing spirit of ecumenicity within the Roman Catholic Church. This spirit was dramatized in the first session of the Second Vatican Council.

The author acknowledges and expresses his debt to all who in any way inspired and encouraged him in this undertaking. He is grateful to Dr. Karl Barth for his wholesome suggestions when the plan of the book was just an idea. The writer has profited much from the constructive suggestions made by the late Father Gustave Weigel, S.J., to whom the whole brief was read. Included in this list must be the name of Dr. Marcus Barth who read the entire manuscript and with whom several sessions were held in oral discussions on many of the main points of the argument and the plan. To Mrs. Maude T. Jackson, my wife, I am greatly indebted for the help and encouragement given. Much of the material in the first draft was dictated to her and she was patient enough to listen for long hours to the reading and re-reading of the manuscript for clarity. For helpful suggestions on structure and organization the author owes much to Dr. Kenny Jackson, his daughter, who read the manuscript over some seven or eight times. Too much cannot be said for the diligence and the sacrificial labor of my private secretary, Mrs. Naomi Mason, who was responsible for taking the dictation and for typing every draft including its final form. While the author acknowledges his indebtedness to all who in any wise influenced his effort or made constructive suggestions, he must take full responsibility for the theological position, general ideas, organization, and conclusions of the book.

J. H. JACKSON

Chicago, Illinois

CONTENTS

I

EXISTING DIFFERENCES IN THE CHRISTIAN CHURCH

1

ORIGIN OF THE PROBLEM

THE CHRISTIAN CHURCH began as a small company of
humble disciples drawn from the same community and the same
cultural level. Their occupations differed; some were fishermen,
some tax collectors, and others held menial jobs. Their interests
merged in their common commitment to Jesus of Nazareth and
His message. The group, then, was fairly homogeneous, for they
had much in common and experienced kinship of interest in the
Kingdom of God. Through the guidance of the Holy Spirit, this
fellowship went from place to place preaching the gospel of the
Kingdom. As they traveled, they left their imprint on every
community visited by winning new disciples and establishing
new centers.

Due to the distance which separated them, members of the
fellowship found it impossible to meet daily or even weekly;
consequently, the fellowship was divided into small groups
according to the communities in which they were located.

Under the leadership and through the missionary efforts of the
Apostle Paul, many of the early local churches were organized.
On his three historic missionary journeys Paul established, nur-
tured, and encouraged independent, local Christian communities.
It is most significant that the man who was later to advance and
to write a theology of Christian unity was himself the pioneer
in establishing so many separate, independent, and local units.
Nevertheless, all of these units were fellowships.

During and after the work of Paul it was natural to speak
both of the church representing the total fellowship and of the

3

churches which represented the fellowship in the respective local communities. These local churches existed to guarantee a more effective working participation of the members of the Christian fellowship. But soon these individual communities developed teachers who advanced their own ideas of the Kingdom, emphasizing certain principles of the gospel of Jesus Christ. Thus did differing ideas emerge in the respective local churches. The letters written by Paul to the local churches were designed not only to nurture and strengthen the believers in the faith, but also to heal breaches, correct errors, and discourage divisions that had appeared in their organizations. In some cases Judaizing teachers had entered, persuading the people that these new Christian communities should adopt and follow much of the ritual, ceremony, and practice that had become a vital part of the religious faith of the Hebrews. Some even taught that Christians should be circumcised as a condition of membership in the Christian fellowship.

In the early church the interpretations of some of the leaders tended toward divisions and differences within the respective fellowships, and many members became followers of these leaders. Paul addressed this issue directly when he wrote to the church at Corinth.

For it hath been declared unto me of you, my brethren, by them which are of the house of Chloe, that there are contentions among you.

Now this I say, that every one of you saith, I am of Paul; and I of Apollos; and I of Cephas; and I of Christ.

Is Christ divided? was Paul crucified for you? or were ye baptized in the name of Paul? (1 Corinthians 1:11-13).

Many of these differences have plagued the life of the church through the centuries in one form or another and are traceable to doctrines, special emphasis on aspects of the same truth, influence of various philosophies and diversified conceptions of the organizational structure of the Christian fellowship. One of the significant points of departure has been the place and function of the officers of the church who are regarded by some as the legitimate and God-ordained representatives of Christ and the church.

When he was converted to Christianity, Constantine at once made Christianity the official religion of the Roman Empire. It is said that by this act the emperor made the state Christian, but the corollary of his act was that he made the church a state institution under imperial control. As an accepted part of the Roman Empire the church prospered and increased in power and authority. The great schism between the eastern and western church came about because the east revolted and refused to accept the authority of the west and the power of the Pope in Rome. The Protestant Reformation of the sixteenth century occasioned further divisions within the organized church and paved the way for the rise of many denominations and sects.

In the course of history another force appeared which contributed to the further break-down of Christian unity. This was the political force known as nationalism which drew some of the loyalty from the empire concept of government and centered it on smaller political units or states.

With the evolution of human society and the development of economic and political life men overcame the ancient feudal system and arrived at a new type of unity. These new groups were held together by a common language, well-defined geographic areas, traditions, economic necessity, and cultural concerns. Their political organizations, economic policies and philosophies were peculiar to their needs and outlooks. They soon developed a love for country and for the country's cause which they described as patriotism. Nationalism became a kind of faith, devotion, and loyalty of the citizens to the state. The state was the great objective for which the citizens lived and for which they would gladly die in times of emergency. Such divisions in human society inevitably had serious effects upon the fellowship called the church of Jesus Christ. In some cases, the church was so aligned with the state that it became a part of, and in fact, wholly identified with the state. Hence, the origin of state churches. Out of the experience of nationalism there developed a wider breach between Christians in different sections of the world.

With the founding of the United States of America, a new kind of nation was born, a nation based not on any one race, nationality, language, or culture, but on a combination of these. The original settlers had come to America from different sections of Europe and, in many cases, from different cultural, economic, political, and religious environments. But they all came in quest of new freedom, new opportunities for living, new economic possibilities, and new religious freedom. America was largely a unique social experiment where peoples of different nations and races and beliefs were brought together in utter commitment to one thing: Freedom. For this reason, many of the divisions among Christians in America may be traced to social, not doctrinal reasons.

This new freedom lent itself to a new individualism that was inclined to look with some degree of suspicion on any authoritarian religion and tended to take the priesthood of all believers most seriously. When one adds to this the influence of the American frontier with its solitude, loneliness and its forced reliance of the individual upon his God, himself, and the forces of nature, one discovers much of the data that helped to shape the American church and American religious life. A Christianity soon emerged that became germane to America and most peculiar to this nation.

Because there were so many varied forces playing upon the lives of men and because they were free to react according to their own choices, the number of different denominations multiplied by the scores so that at one time there were 213 different Christian denominations in the United States of America.[1] These

---

[1] William Warren Sweet, *The Story of Religion in America* (New York, Harper & Brother, 1930), p. 1. Dr. Sweet based his findings on the last religious census that was taken prior to 1930. *Cf. The Yearbook of American Churches* (1963). According to the religious census appearing in the *Yearbook* there are now 258 religious bodies in the United States.

denominations were based on certain peculiar emphases and were supported by scriptural texts to give the proper authority to the emphasis embraced, for it was the custom in those days to find a passage of scripture to justify the existence of each Christian sect. But many of these divisions basically were due to the social forces playing upon the minds of the people.

One illustration of the influence of social forces is the rise of different Christian groups based on their reactions to the issue of slavery. Most of the American churches put the free men in one class before God, and slaves in another. In those houses of worship where slaves were permitted, there was a segregated section reserved for them. When the fullness of time came, the emancipated slaves reacted positively against their experiences in the segregated churches and declared themselves free in the sight of God. They organized their own churches based not on a pattern of segregation out of which they had come but on "THE WHOSOEVER WILL" of the gospel of Jesus Christ.

Slaveholders and others interested in the success of the institution of slavery influenced churches of which they were members to become bulwarks of this cursed institution. In some cases churches divided and new ones formed according to those who believed or did not believe in the practice of slavery. Many writers have detailed the tragic story of the divisions of churches in matters of slavery. William Warren Sweet says:

The most important and far-reaching of the schisms in the American churches were caused by Negro slavery, and the effects of that bitter contest in the churches are still with us. This gives American Christianity a peculiarity of its own. . . . It was not until church members had become wealthy cotton growers, that the church ceased to denounce the institution. At the adoption of the Constitution all of the churches were unanimous in their opposition to slavery; by the opening of the Civil War the churches had become the chief bulwark of American slavery.[2]

[2] *Ibid.*, pp. 6-7.

The author points out in another place, that when new cotton growers developed in America and new demands were made for cotton, both the price of cotton and the price of slaves took a tremendous leap.

Between 1791 and 1795, 5,200,000 pounds of cotton was produced. Between 1826 and 1830, 307,244,400 pounds. In 1820 cotton constituted twenty-two per cent of the nation's exports, in 1860 fifty-seven percent. In 1790 good Negroes might be purchased for three hundred dollars; the same Negro in 1830 would bring $1,200.00 and in 1860 $1,500 to $2,000.00. In other words slavery was more important economically both to the south and to the nation between 1830 and 1860 than it was between 1775 and 1830.[3]

The economic influence of slavery affected the churches to such a degree that they became the actual defenders of this cruel and godless institution. This is clearly revealed by James G. Birney in his famous book, *The American Churches: The Bulwark of American Slavery.*

There is a record of church divisions based on the issue of slavery. In 1845 the Baptists of America were split into northern and southern on the question of slavery. The Southern Baptist Convention was organized May 8, 1845.

History testifies to similarly tragic divisions among those who claimed to represent one Lord and one faith. Serious conflicts, tragic bloodshed and other evils have resulted from differences among those who named the name of Jesus Christ. Brother has been against brother, believer has imprisoned believer, and Christians have come forward to crush and to kill fellow believers, with whom they differed on points of interpretation, philosophy and theology. Some have acted as if they thought the reign of the Prince of Peace could be established by the use of the sword. The divisions themselves were tragic enough, but

[3] *Ibid.*, p. 6.

the conflicts and the persecutions that resulted have left shameful scars on the life and history of the Christian church.

When the churches in Europe and the United States sought to respond to the great commission, "Go ye into all the world," they went to foreign fields under the authority and guidance of their respective denominations. The piety and zeal of the conscientious missionaries were somehow fettered by the rules and policies of their denominations. It seems that for a season the sinning churches were unconscious of the tensions and misunderstanding that denominationalism was occasioning for the new converts and for the so-called heathens to whom they had sent the message of salvation. The questions and the expressions of disappointment over such grave divisions among Christians eventually shocked missionaries and sinning churches into a consciousness of the gravity of the sins of division and the scandal of Christian conflict.

As denominations sought to justify their differences, they became more and more aware of the perils of the tragic divisions among the churches. It was not long before the churches repented of their sins of competition and repudiated the modern scandal of their division. They looked forward to the day when such errors could be overcome and the conflicts would be lost in a broader and more constructive field of cooperation. The minds of scholars and theologians became engaged in the quest for "a way out." The devout prayerfully sought a remedy for the diseases of division. The prayer of Jesus that all believers would be one, and Paul's doctrine of the church as the body of Christ, had been denied by divisions. Here was a great conflict. Here was the church acting as a family torn with strife and standing as a house divided against itself, denying in practice what it affirmed in theory.

In order to overcome the difficulties and solve the problems at hand, many voices were lifted and many solutions proposed. Some dreamed of organic union, others of the complete annihilation of all differences and the development of a sacred sameness among all Christians and all churches.

At this point, we would raise this question: "Are all differences among believers indefensible, or can there be found within the Christian fellowship differences that are both reasonable and defensible which in no way hinder Christian cooperation or jeopardize the constructive life of the Christian community and the fellowship of all believers"?

2

DIFFERENCES:
DEFENSIBLE AND INDEFENSIBLE

THERE ARE serious differences among the various Christian denominations on many issues, some doctrinal and theological. For the purpose of our discussion we have elected to divide these into two classes, namely; those that are defensible and those that are indefensible. In the approach to the problem of Christian unity, sameness is not necessarily the answer. There are some differences that are both logical and defensible; there can be a case made for them because they are justifiable and necessary. On the other hand, there are other differences which are not defensible, not necessary, and cannot be justified.

The church as we know it is comprised of human beings. The believers who are the members of the church are not angels, but ordinary men and women. They bring with them some of their natural gifts that are not basically changed. Even after regeneration there is much that is left the same. The believers take these things that are not changed into the church with them, and these qualities remain with them as long as they are living creatures, having their influence on the church and leaving their mark on the fellowship of the believers. Let us note some of these briefly.

According to educational psychology, each normal person has an intelligence quotient that he keeps through life without any appreciable change. A converted man may have his mind quickened, his heart changed and his life more completely integrated by the ideals of Jesus Christ, so much so that he becomes a new creation. But this great spiritual revolution does not alter his I.Q. The capacity for learning is a given which discipline and education can do little or nothing to change. If people with an average I.Q. are told the story of the Christ, they cannot comprehend more than their powers will allow. They cannot give out what they have not received, and they cannot receive more than their capacities will permit. Becoming a member of the Christian fellowship is not predicated on the I.Q. of the believer. It matters not how high the I.Q. may be, or how close to the average; the message of Jesus is still to "THE WHOSO-EVER WILL."

The story of the talents in the New Testament does not refer to one's I.Q. but rather is designed to show that the man who exercises his spiritual gifts will increase his spiritual strength. It further shows that God simply requires of men that they use the talents they have. The constant I.Q. will reflect itself in what individuals and groups can both receive and share in the way of knowledge. Not every believer is expected to write great theological tracts or to build cathedrals or to produce great works of art, but he is expected to serve God in the light of his own gifts, capacities, and mental powers. The expression of his testimony will differ in the light of his God-given equipment, but it is no less valuable in the sight of God than that of those who possess great mental capacities. Humble believers in Christ Jesus are not required to imitate or to produce the same type of mental image in their worship and testimony as the more gifted. And conversely, the more gifted are not limited in their worship, religious experiences and insights to the level of the less gifted. Each is to hear according to his God-given capacities to hear and to testify in earnest with the equipment that God has given.

Just as there is a difference in the capacity to hear and in the gift to testify, so there may be a difference in testimony and, in some cases, in the formulation of Christian ideas and ideals. These differences do not warrant the organization of different factions or denominations. People with different talents may live in the same church fellowship, worship the same God and render their services unto their Maker. Christ is not a Christ of the high I.Q.'s alone or a Savior of the mentally retarded. He comes to seek and to save the lost. He does not require that the mentally gifted dissipate their powers in order to be Christian, but He requires that they consecrate their powers to His service, surrendering all that they are and have to His name and His glory.

Paul recognized the fact of differences among the members of the church and supported these differences. Said he:

For as we have many members in one body, and all members have not the same office: So we, being many, are one body in Christ, and every one members one of another. Having then gifts differing according to the grace that is given to us, whether prophecy, let us prophesy according to the proportion of faith; or ministry, let us wait on our ministering: or he that teaches, on teaching; or he that exhorteth, on exhortation. . . . (Romans 12:4-8).

The Apostle sees the variety of gifts but labors not to reduce them to sameness. He calls upon those who listen to him to follow the voice of God and to employ their gifts in the service of the Kingdom of God. In another letter, he re-emphasizes this same great truth, urging the members of the church to accept the fact of their differences and to make wise and constructive use of their respective gifts. (*Cf.* 1 Corinthians 12:7). These defensible differences are in the realm of talents, capacities and gifts, but the constant or the reigning sameness is represented both by the Holy Spirit, the one Lord of life and the one God, the Father of all. Our Apostle says:

Now there are diversities of gifts, but the same Spirit. And there are differences of administrations, but the same Lord. And there are diversities of operations, but it is the same God which worketh all in all (1 Corinthians 12:4-6).

Once the fact of such differences among members of the Christian fellowship is accepted, it is impossible to labor for and to expect a sameness in worship and testimony. For these differences occur on the level of talents and gifts. But undergirding all of them should be the Holy Spirit, Jesus Christ, the Lord of Life, and God the Father. All differences in the Christian fellowship are defensible so long as they rest on the fact of the eternal truth of the spiritual order. This teaches us tolerance in differences and benevolence and love among all the members in the body of Christ.

As we observe the historic struggle of man in the building of civilizations and in the organization of the various social structures, including the different living religions and the various philosophies of life, we can note what I have elected to call in this connection, an *intelligence tendency*. That is, certain minds tend to react in a certain pattern. This tendency is so strong that it may be described as the mind of a certain people in a given culture. When we observe the ancient Hebrews we discover that there was a tendency to interpret the whole of life in terms of a religious outlook. There was, in reality, no certain distinction between what we might call the political state and the religious life of the people. Since they tended towards the grouping of all the parts into one meaningful whole, their conception of a political organization was one in which God was the Supreme Ruler and all laws had to be derived from the divine command, and any earthly rulers whether they be kings or judges, had to receive their authority from God. This Jewish theocracy recognized no such thing as a secular government, and hence for them there was no distinction between church and state. The simple matters of diet, as well as the discipline for families, were related to their idea of God and became a part of their religious concepts. Whenever it looked out upon the world, the Hebrew mind saw evidences of the presence of God and His creative acts. If we speak of their reaction to the stars and to the heavens as their astronomy, the conclusion must be that the astronomy of the ancient Hebrews was interpreted with an orientation towards their God. It was not the tendency of the Hebrew mind to isolate the heavens as an object of science and deal with the mysteries of the stars and the planets independently of the idea of God. For them the open heavens were public declarations of the glory of God, and the multitude of stars were shining demonstrations of the work of His hand. "The heavens declare the glory of God and the firmament sheweth forth His handiwork."

Among the ancient Greeks there was a different *intelligence tendency*. The Greek mind tended towards speculation and sought an explanation for the meaning of things that appeared. The Greeks sought an answer to the basic question: why? Their concern was the why of life, the why of human existence, and the why of the great mental and moral forces in the life of mankind. In this chain of interrogations we have the raw material for philosophy. It is the Greek mind that has produced philosophy. Wherever this type of mind touches the problem of life and religion, there is speculation and there is the call to reason together, to seek by the process of thought and human logic to arrive at the knowledge of truth, at the meaning of the origin and destiny of human life, and at the source of all being.

Just as the idea of God in the Greek framework of thought would be different from the idea of God as advanced in the minds of the ancient Hebrews, so among the ancient Romans there was still a different *intelligence tendency*, one designed to catalog and organize the forces of life and society. In their quest for laws to regulate the social order, the Romans became the pioneers in this field. The Roman Empire in its vast accomplishments was a product of the Roman mind. When this mind approached the problems of religion, the natural results were observed at best in societies and organizations. This was just as natural for the Roman mind as was speculation for the Greek mind or theocratic thinking for the Hebrews.

In the United States of America we have evidence of much

that has been borrowed from the Hebrews, Greeks, and Romans. America as a young nation naturally would show signs of its kinship and dependence on the more mature nations from which her Founding Fathers came. Yet observation reveals an *intelligence tendency* peculiar to the United States. It is a kind of practical approach to the problems of life. The American mind is concerned with results, that is, getting things done. It has a kind of activism that is concerned with achievements and, at times, seems obsessed with short-term goals.

This mind gives birth to a cult of progress stimulated and inspired by a process philosophy. In the context of this philosophy, the present is not only a product of the past but a basis for the anticipated future. "What was" somewhat fades into insignificance in the light of "what is," and "what is now" is subject to and relative to "what is yet to come." With no stubborn past on which to anchor and to bind the various forces that play upon the present and with the call of the unknown future, it is not strange that the American mind lends itself to a multiplicity of forces and processes. Hence, there is peculiar to America an individualism that not only takes lightly and—in some cases—is in open revolt against any form of authority but also tends to accept as final, the decisions and values supported by a majority vote. In brief, this is the American *intelligence tendency,* and because of it, many different types of religious ideas and patterns of thought have been produced.

We have these four patterns of thought; there are many others that could be mentioned. These suffice to illustrate the differences that various groups may bring to the religious experience. The response that follows the reception of the gospel of Jesus Christ is in a measure determined by the mind tendency that one brings with him to the hour of worship. A contemplative mind will tend toward the mystical elements and proclaim them as the message of Jesus Christ. These different mind-sets will find their expression in theology, organization, and worship.

A uniform program of worship in any church has many advantages. But because of differences in the mental and emotional tendencies of the people, it has the disadvantage of missing many would-be worshipers at the level of their deepest needs and longings. Therefore, it is essential that in a program of worship, where men of different backgrounds and different intellectual tendencies are brought together, there should somehow be a varied program to meet, at least in part, these varied needs.

The next defensible difference is in the category of expression. Each nation possesses its own peculiar language. This is a gift of nature that religion of itself cannot reverse or change. When men of various nationalities have had their experience of Christ, they must rely on their language in their efforts to express this deeply moving experience. Few can express themselves as well in one language as in another. Most rely upon the use of their mother tongues to express the feelings of their souls. However miraculous and moving the experience, man needs familiar symbols and images in order to relate what has transpired within, and those with whom he communicates must be able to understand and interpret these pictures and symbols. I am not ready to conclude that the best way to advance the work of the Kingdom of God is to reduce all languages to one and to demand that all men speak a common language. While this would greatly simplify the problem of universal communication, it is not essential to the advancement of the Kingdom of God.

Three defensible differences that may be found in the Christian church have been mentioned. It is not essential that all Christians have the same I.Q., the same *intelligence tendency*, or the same language in order to experience the desired Christian unity and fellowship. Nature has ordained and sustained certain differences in human beings; these are glorious gifts. They are divine blessings and lend themselves to the possibility of a harmony with a greater depth and wealth than uniformity could ever bring. Defensible differences may stand, for the real kinship of believers rests not in a labored sameness, but in the deeper realms of the spiritual life. On the other hand, what has been said about defensible differences does not by any means justify the existence of a multitude of divisions within the Christian fellowship. There are some differences within the Christian church that are not necessary and are indefensible both by reason and by the righteous judgment of God.

The universal cry among Christians for a world-wide fellowship and the historic, vital efforts to overcome the many divisions within the family of Jesus Christ tell us that not only religious thinkers but also humble believers in all denominations are aware that there are differences among us that reflect discredit on the Christ whom we adore and that tend to negate the positive message of His cross. These indefensible differences should be erased from the records of contemporary religious life. We should humbly seek forgiveness for the scars of the past that have been occasioned by them. Let us note briefly some of these indefensible differences.

First, any defensible difference that is so interpreted as to inflame the connecting joints and vital tissues of a Christian fellowship becomes indefensible by that interpretation. Any natural differences that nature and nature's God have given to us that are used to limit the universal claims of the gospel of Jesus Christ are not only indefensible but become a hindrance and a curse to His message. Any surface differences that are so interpreted as to determine the fitness of a person to become a member of the fellowship of Christ are indefensible. And yet when we read the story of the church from the day of Pentecost until now, we see scores and scores of barriers designed to divide and to confuse the people of God. Walls of partition have been erected, separating the people of God. Impassable gulfs have been made between the God of Jesus Christ and many humble souls who thirst for the fresh waters of salvation.

Some of these indefensible differences occur in the field of theological thought. The chief doctrinal ground for the schism between the Greek and Roman Churches came over the Latin word, "filioque," which means "and from the Son." This clause was added to the Latin version of the Nicene Creed at the Council of Toledo, indicating that the procession of the Holy Spirit is from the Father and the Son. The Greek thinkers objected to this addition and contended that the Holy Spirit came from the Father only. As we look upon this difference in the light of history and by the inspiration of truth, we may see clearly that this difference could have remained as a part of the thought pattern of these branches of the Christian church without causing a schism if they could have concentrated on the fact that they were so much agreed that the Holy Spirit had come to them as a living reality. The difference as to the relation of the Son to the Father need not separate those who are committed to the work of the Father through the inspiration of the Holy Spirit.

Another question that requires much thought is whether or not the final separation between the Roman Catholic Church and the Greek Orthodox Church over the growing power of the Pope in Rome was a sufficient difference in concept of authority to occasion the separation between these believers. The same may be said of the new nationalism that sprang up with the birth of modern states. While one can admit that the divisions of the peoples of the world into races and nations is natural and defensible, an interpretation of the Christian religion based on these things is not. Furthermore, what may be said of nations may also be said of the races of men.

In the United States of America, we had, for the first time, churches organized according to race. With the institution of American slavery, masters sought to combine the authority and the privilege of slave owners with the blessings of Christ in fellowship and communion. Instead of seeking to free their slaves many masters sought to lift their slaves and the pattern of segregation into their Christian churches. There were certain segregated sections reserved for the slaves where they might sit and hear the pastors of the white masters preach the gospel of redemption. This of course was not only an open sin against divine grace but also a revolt against the universality of the gospel and an open rebellion against the message of the Cross of Christ.

It was not too long before the self-respect, the manhood, and the insights of the slaves led them to question the sincerity of their masters and to doubt the veracity of a religion that allowed a man to bind others in chains and to deal with them as he would animals that could be sold or even bartered for material gain. The personalities and the souls of slaves were so disregarded and disrespected that on one occasion a slave owner willed that some of the slaves she owned would be sold at her death to assist in the education of Indians.[1]

When they revolted against this unholy alliance of slave owner and religion, the slaves began to think in terms of a common worship among themselves. This small beginning prior to the days of emancipation took on significant proportions in subsequent years. Thus, beginning with the slave and continuing with the freedmen, the chasm deepened between the segregating believer and the segregated believer, so that in time a form of Christianity was established in America based on race. Many of the masters, ex-masters and their children labored to keep their churches pure from the presence and participation of men and women of color. On the other hand, men and women of color having lost confidence in the religious integrity of their former masters, sought to establish their own churches and to worship God under their own vine and fig tree according to the dictates of their consciences.

Negro churches were established as early as 1776. The most famous of these early churches was the First African Baptist

---

[1] James C. Birney, *The American Church The Bulwark of American Slavery* (New York, Parker Pillsbury, 1885), p. 11. See the story of the will of Ann Pray.

Church established in 1787 in Savannah, Georgia, by the Rev. Abraham Marshall, who was white, and the Rev. Jesse Peters, who was a Negro. Andrew Bryan, a slave of Jonathan Bryan, was the first preacher. In 1792, after suffering much persecution, Bryan began the erection of a church building of his own in the city of Savannah, Georgia, which became the First Bryan Baptist Church. It was not until 1836 that the Providence Baptist Association, the first Baptist association of Negroes, was organized in Ohio. In 1880, the National Baptist Convention was organized at Montgomery, Alabama.

But the first organization of Negro churches as an independent denomination had its origin at St. George's Church in Philadelphia when an attempt was made to move Richard Allen and some other members of the congregation from their accustomed seats in the body of the church to the gallery. They objected and walked out of the church, and on April 17, 1787, Richard Allen and Absalon Jones formed the Free African Society, a sort of a union or community Negro church formed without regard to religious tenets providing the members lived an orderly and sober life. Feeling the need of a creed and a staid form of organization, in 1790, Richard Allen with a few followers withdrew from the fellowship and started an independent Methodist Church. In 1816, a conference of other independent Negro Methodist Churches was held, and the African Methodist Episcopal Church was founded with Richard Allen as first Bishop. In 1796, colored members of the Methodist Episcopal Church in New York elected to form a separate congregation, which was to become known as the African Methodist Episcopal Zion Church. It was in 1820 that colored Methodist congregations in New York, New Haven, Long Island, and Philadelphia severed their connection with the old mother church and united to form the historic Zion Church. Negro members of the Methodist Church remained within the folds of said Church until after the Civil War. But in 1866 the Southern Methodist Church authorized the colored members at their own request to organize a separate congregation under their own preachers. These denominations were the pioneers in the formation of what is now known in America as the Negro church.

The tragedy is not alone in the fact that such differences were hardened into fixed separations between believers in the primitive days of servitude, but it is most tragic that at this present hour, in spite of the enlightenment of science, the discipline of philosophy and the bright light of truth from the message and sacrificial life and death of Jesus, there are churches, scores and hundreds of them in the United States of America, which still believe that a church based on race is acceptable to a righteous God, and that a theology of color and caste can convey the true doctrine of the Christ of the Cross.

In the midst of such a scandal of religion and in spite of the darkness of ignorance and superstition that cast their shadows across the Christian path, there are some devout Christians in all the churches of the United States of America that believe with all their hearts that there is no place in the Church of Jesus Christ for the pattern of racial segregation and for the curse of human discrimination. It is no sin against the church of Jesus Christ when men and women of like tastes and similar religious experiences are drawn together in local units and in fellowship based on common desires, so long as they always understand that they are members of the one body of the Lord Jesus Christ, and that it can never be their power or their purpose to erect barriers to keep others of different races and different nationalities from seeking membership in their Christian fraternity.

These and many other differences within our Christian family are indefensible, for they cannot stand the test of truth. Neither can they survive the scrutiny of the Spirit of God and the voice of Jesus Christ when He summons all men to come to Him for guidance, comfort and redemption.

However, we are beginning to recognize more clearly that even in differences there are many similarities. A comparative study of some of the historic differences between the Roman Catholic Church and Protestant Churches will reveal this fact.

3

SOME SIMILARITIES IN DIFFERENCES

THAT THERE ARE many differences between the Roman
Catholic Church and the Protestant Churches of the world cannot be doubted, for history has proclaimed these dissimilarities,
and time has preserved them. Any student of church history
can, without too much effort, tabulate deviations in dogma, organization and worship, *ad infinitum,* which distinguish these
bodies one from the other. No degree of compromise or apology
can destroy these existing facts.

The purpose here is not to minimize these differences. Nor
is it to seek by means of language and logic to explain away
what the facts have affirmed. It is not the purpose at this point
to attempt an easy road of reconciliation between the Roman
Catholic Church and those separated brethren who departed
from the Roman Church in the sixteenth century under the
leadership of Martin Luther. There is no easy road in matters
of readjustment, reestablishment of cooperation, or rebuilding a
broken fellowship. Instead, the intent of this chapter is to select
at least two of the historic differences between Roman Catholics
and Protestants which have appeared on the doctrinal level and
make a brief examination of these differences to see if there be
elements that are similar. The two dogmas selected for this
purpose are papal infallibility and Mariolatry, or the veneration
of the Virgin Mary, the Mother of Jesus.

When one considers the dogma of papal infallibility, he discovers first that the doctrine of infallibility is a sanction or an
authority residing in an utterance, a person, or an institution

rendering it or him incapable of error. The idea in general is a particular instance of a dogmatic conception of Divine Guidance. God cannot err. His knowledge and His Holy Will will not permit Him to make mistakes. Consequently, any utterance of God must be infallible. The Roman Catholic Church in its teachings emphasizes the divine authority of the Holy Scriptures and of the Holy Church. But both in theory and in practice throughout its long history the infallibility of the Roman Church has been put to the front, for the Church alone is divinely authorized to determine the prescribed lists of inspired books. It has the exclusive right and authority to infallibly declare the true meaning of the Scriptures. This requires some official spokesman or some undisputed voice that can become the voice of the Church itself. In the judgment of the Church Fathers it was not practical to leave such responsibility in the hands of the majority members of a Council of the Church. They finally came to the position that the unequivocal voice representing the Church should be located in the Supreme Roman Pontiff himself. Thus, the foundation was well laid for the dogma of papal infallibility.

Prior to 1870 there were divergent views within the Roman Catholic Church regarding this dogma of the infallibility of the Pope. When the First Vatican Council was assembled December 8, 1869 by Pope Pius IX, there was a division of opinion as to whether a discussion on papal infallibility should be included on the agenda. Since the Council had been called to consider many doctrinal and social problems arising out of the discussion of the papal Syllabus of 1864, it was impossible to dismiss papal infallibility which was one of the pressing questions of the times. Fifteen days after the conference opened, Archbishops Dechamps and Manning and others launched a campaign to define papal infallibility. They were successful in their efforts, and more than five hundred other Fathers attending the Council subscribed to their plea. The minority of 136 Church Fathers soon discovered that their efforts were futile and they saw the topic of papal infallibility added to the schema (the Church of Christ). The dogma of papal infallibility was approved by a large majority of the Church Fathers present. It declared that when the Roman Pontiff speaks ex cathedra, that is, when as pastor and teacher of all Christians he defines a doctrine regarding faith and morals to be held by the universal Church, by virtue of his supreme apostolic authority and by the divine assistance promised to him in Blessed Peter, he is in possession of that infallibility with which the Divine Redeemer wills that the Church should be endowed when defining doctrine regarding faith and morals. After the vote of the Council, Pope Pius IX immediately promulgated the dogma of the infallibility of the Pope. There were some who refused to accept the dogma but later changed their positions by signing their acceptance of the Council's decree. There were others, however, in Germany who led a movement to resist the Vatican Decree and won supporters in several nations. As a result, in Germany, Switzerland, Austria, the Netherlands, and some other countries, over 150,000 persons joined in opposition to the decree of papal infallibility. This led to the formation of what was later known as the Old Catholic Church. But since the First Vatican Council of 1870 the doctrine of papal infallibility has been one of the primary dogmas of the Roman Catholic Church.

A careful study of this doctrine clearly reveals that it does not proclaim that the Pope is beyond mistakes or that he is, as a man, infallible at all times. The Pope as a man and as a citizen is subject to the limitations peculiar to human nature, but when he is exercising the office of pastor and teacher of Christians within the Roman Catholic Church, what he says concerning faith and morals is infallible. According to this doctrine, when he receives the keys of the kingdom (authority) and uses these keys by divine inspiration and divine direction, the Pope cannot make a mistake while dealing with matters that regard faith and morals.

The actions, the words, and the attitude of Pope John XXIII

on the occasion of opening the Second Vatican Council, October 11, 1962, clearly revealed how much he relied upon God and not upon his own self-sufficiency. When he knelt in prayer before the altar with bowed head, he, by that very act, confessed his dependency on a Power greater than himself. He was seeking divine guidance and was in quest of the will and the way of God as he applied himself to the task at hand.

In a statement before the Observers and Guests in his palace, Pope John XXIII demonstrated and revealed his spirit of humility. Said he:

> In so far as it concerns my humble person, I would not like to claim any special inspiration. I content myself with the sound doctrine which teaches that everything comes from God. In this sense I have considered this idea of a Council which began on the 11th of October to be a heavenly inspiration.

Here Pope John XXIII does not lay claim to self-sufficiency; neither does he boast of a self-reliance that excludes the need for the guidance of the Holy Spirit. For him infallibility is not a human virtue, nor is it the genius or the possession of any man without the guidance and inspiration that comes from God. F. J. Sheed teaches the same general truth regarding papal infallibility in the following words:

> A pope does not necessarily by some miracle know the whole of Catholic doctrine, the answer to every doctrinal question that could be raised. The Church, of course, is overruled by the Providence of God, and if some teaching were at a given moment essential for the Church's well-being, God would see that we had it. But I am concerned here with the human machinery, so to speak, of infallibility. And it remains true that what he does not know he cannot teach. But in no case can he teach what is wrong: for God will not let him, lest we, the members of the Church, be led into error.[1]

[1] Sheed, F. J., *A Map of Life* (New York, Sheed & Ward, 1933), pp. 75-76.

This, then, is a brief summary of the doctrine of papal infallibility. At a supreme moment when confronted with a supreme task—a task which is in the field of things moral and spiritual—and when the supreme gift of God comes to influence and to direct a committed servant of His in the execution of this task, it is at that point that there is infallibility, that there is promulgation beyond error.

In this discussion the writer has striven for objectivity and has tried to allow the Roman Church to speak for itself and to define its own dogma as she sees it. We have not affirmed or denied; we have simply stated what the doctrine is. As a Protestant, the writer has striven to follow the interpretation not of Protestant theologians, but of Catholic theologians. For if we are to grasp the significance of a dogma we must first of all make sure that we understand what that dogma means in the framework of the theological scheme in which it is found.

It is clear to every student of Protestant thought that Protestantism strongly objects to the dogma of papal infallibility, because it rejects the infallibility of the church that grants the authority to the pope himself. But our purpose here is not to analyze Protestant arguments against the Roman Catholic doctrine of papal infallibility. Rather, we are to inquire of Protestant thinkers and to probe into Protestant theology to find if there be there any kind of doctrine of infallibility. If so, how does it relate itself to the views held by the Roman Catholic Church?

Protestants have held to the idea of the infallibility of the Scriptures. The Bible is God's Holy Book. It is the treasure house of truth without mixture or error. As Paul has pointed out:

All scripture is given by inspiration of God, and is profitable for doctrine, for reproof, for correction, for instruction in righteousness (2 Timothy 3:16).

Scholarship has removed many traditional concepts concerning the origin and growth of the Bible. The scientific and the historic methods have been employed in an attempt to lead students of the Bible to a greater appreciation of its basic values and truths. Scholars have long since drawn a distinction between levels of ethical content found both in sections of the Old as well as the New Testaments. But basically, Protestant scholars and thinkers still regard the Bible as the primary source book of the Christian religion, especially the New Testament. It is on this source book that the church depends for its insights, its knowledge, and its guidance in moral and spiritual matters. If one destroys faith in the Holy Scriptures, he destroys the foundation of the Christian church and is left groping in the darkness without the hope of ever seeing the light. Protestants believe that prophets are inspired of God and at the moment of inspiration they hear His voice, they learn His will for the task at hand, and they see the path on which they must set their pilgrim feet. These men of God spoke and acted as they were moved by the Spirit of God. Their messages were not the results of human speculation, unaided genius, and the logical comprehension of facts. They were God-filled men, God-inspired men, and God-directed men.

When the great apostles and preachers of the New Testament proclaimed "thus saith the Lord," they spoke under the compulsion of a new life and by the guidance of divine inspiration. It was not their story; it was God's story. It was not their gospel; it was the gospel of Jesus Christ. The inspiration given is designed to make the man of God infallible.

That the man of God may be perfect, thoroughly furnished unto all good works (2 Timothy 3:17).

The great Apostle Paul did not allow himself to take credit for the gospel he preached, nor did he trace his gospel authority to any school of prophets or any academy of religious teachers. The gospel he preached came as a result of the Christ who had been revealed in him, and once the Christ was revealed in him it was not necessary for him to seek the advice of men as to what Christ required of him.

> But when it pleased God . . . to reveal his Son in me . . . I conferred not with flesh and blood (Galatians 1:15-16).

These brief statements represent the Protestant conception of inspiration, guidance, and participation of the inspired ones in the declaration of divine truth and in the work of the propagation of the gospel.

Protestants have accepted the position that much of the teachings regarding the Christ and much of the heart of the gospel, including the ideals of the Kingdom of God, were first set forth as oral testimony; later the oral testimony was written on parchment and step-by-step the written word became the treasured possession of the Christian church. In the process of translating the Bible into the vernacular, there were scribes who with their own hands copied the message as they translated it from the original into the vernacular. When we say the Bible is infallible, we are compelled to believe that the religious pioneers who transcribed the oral tradition into a written text and those who translated the original into the vernacular have given the generation following them the message originally given by the Holy Spirit. When we present the fact of the inspired book, we are forced to accept the existence of inspired men; if we accept inspired men who gave us an infallible book, we must accept infallible moments in the lives of inspired men without whom the infallible book would be an impossibility.

In the Roman Catholic Church, when there was a need for a voice to deal with an infallible Church, the Pope was selected as that infallible voice. This was for particular moments in the history of the Church and in the history of his own life and service. In the Protestant Church there is an infallible book, called the Bible, and men with inspired and infallible moments have given us this book through the guidance of God the Holy Spirit. Here we are not dealing with the proof of the spiritual validity of inspiration. Nor are we concerned here about how God in His wisdom used corrupt, mortal men to deal with the mysteries of His eternal gospel. We have simply discussed the Protestant doctrine of infallibility and the Roman Catholic dogma of infallibility to show the close kinship between the two.

Another doctrine that divides Roman Catholics and Protestants regards the veneration of the Virgin Mary. It is a dogma of the Roman Catholic Church that Mary, the Mother of Jesus, gave birth to a Son by divine intervention and inspiration. The Virgin Mother was sinless, and her virgin life was a gift from God in preparation for the coming of His Son into the world. The conception of Jesus in a virgin's womb was a miracle and through the grace of God, Mary was so endowed that she brought into the world a Son who knew no sin. Mary was not only pure in her life and in her birth but also at the first instance of her conception was preserved immaculate from the stain of original sin by a singular grace and privilege granted her by Almighty God through the merits of Christ Jesus, Saviour of Mankind. She was sometimes described by the Greek word *"theotokos,"* which means "God-bearer" or "Mother of God."

The Virgin Mary has been called the Mediatress. By this the Roman Church does not seek to distract from the office of mediator as exercised by Christ Himself. Mary mediates between Christ and mankind as she did at Cana in Galilee when the wine gave out. (See John 2:3). Furthermore, Mary is considered as Co-Redemptress based on St. Luke 1:38: "Let it be done to me according to thy word." The Virgin therefore had a share in the work of redemption by being the agent and the first cradle in which the sacred infant slept.

The respect for Mary in the scheme of salvation has grown and her place in the theology of the Roman Catholic Church has somewhat expanded, and she has been granted a special status by the doctrine of her Assumption. Pope Pius XII made this dogma official in 1950 declaring "that the Immaculate Mother of God, the ever Virgin Mary, when the course of her earthly life was run, was assumed in body and in soul to heavenly glory." Some thinkers say that the Virgin Mary has served to symbolize the redemption of the life of nature and to provide a bridge between Christianity and those religions of nature that have spoken of this redemption. Mary has also symbolized the nobility of womanhood. In our estimation of womanhood, our point of departure is no longer Eve in the Garden of Eden, but Mary, the Mother of Jesus. There is a statement in the New Testament which seems to have been a true prophecy regarding the universal respect of motherhood as found in Mary the Mother of Jesus: ". . . behold, from hence forth all generations shall call me blessed" (St. Luke 1:48).

When one turns to Protestant life, teachings, and practice to see if there be any aspect of Protestant life or any celebrations that are in any way similar in devotion to what we find in the Roman Catholic's devotion to the Virgin Mary, one discovers that there is in the Protestant Church a respect and veneration of motherhood, not as found in the Virgin Mary alone, but as found in each individual mother. In 1907, there was inaugurated what is now called Mother's Day. In 1914, the Congress of the United States of America officially recognized and approved the second Sunday in May as Mother's Day. This day is generally observed in the United States and elsewhere to some extent. We have not written any theology of motherhood, but we have written songs in which her virtues are recounted and her glorious life celebrated. The praise ascribed to her on this special day which is included in the calendar of Protestant churches reminds one of a form of worship. On this day the sermons preached are not on the love of God or on the love of Jesus Christ, but on the love of mother. A stanza of a hymn indicates how closely we come to worshipping mother on Mother's Day:

> Faith of our mothers living yet
> In cradle song and bed time prayer,
> In nursery love and fireside love
> Thy presence still pervade the air.
> Faith of our mothers living still
> We will be true to thee till death.

The praise of motherhood and the celebration of her love as a gift of God both to her family and to society is honorable and laudable. But there is a danger in giving to mother a special day of worship in the program of the church. The danger is there might develop a tendency to ascribe to motherhood gifts and graces that can only come from God. Mother, as an agent of creation and as one dedicated to the love and care of growing human beings, is still a servant of God. She is in reality God's creature, and we must not fall into the error of worshiping the creature more than the Creator. But our purpose here is not to evaluate or to analyse the psychology of Mother's Day but rather to point out an existing kinship between Protestants' reaction to mother and the Roman Catholic's veneration of Mary.

CONTENT AND CONTAINER

WE CANNOT FORGET one of the impressive, though brief, parables of Jesus in His attempt to correct the misguided thoughts of the Pharisees and to lead them into a deeper appreciation of His mission and His message. Said He to them:

No man putteth a piece of new cloth unto an old garment, for that which is put in to fill it up taketh from the garment, and the rent is made worse. Neither do men put new wine into old bottles: else the bottles break, and the wine runneth out, and the bottles perish: but they put new wine into new bottles, and both are preserved (Matthew 9:16-17).

Here Jesus draws a line between content and container. The content was the new wine; the containers were the bottles. Wine cannot be kept in crates, in sacks, or in sieves but must be kept in wine skins or in bottles. These bottles, as containers, must be strong enough to hold the wine and durable enough to resist the chemical reaction of fermenting wine. Otherwise the bottles will perish and the wine will be lost. Jesus is teaching in this parable that containers must be of sufficient strength both to contain and to hold the content. If not, the container and the content will be lost.

Ideas are like liquids. They cannot be carried without a container. Ideas need vehicles, substances require forms; living and dynamic thoughts—if they are to have an abiding place in the attitudes, motives, and deeds of the people—must flow into social patterns. These patterns must be acceptable and understandable among the people to whom they are presented. In the case of a spoken language, the syllables, words, and sentences represent the containers.

The late Dean Shailer Mathews of the Divinity School of the University of Chicago made much of the idea of social patterns in the field of theology. It was his contention that theological thought to be meaningful must be expressed in the current social patterns of the times. Furthermore he maintained that we must not confuse the one with the other. The social pattern was essential as a vehicle of expression or as the container in which the content was placed.

In every case, with the possible exception of consubstantiality, the doctrines in Christianity are not metaphysic. They are really patterns derived from that total social life with which it is the business of the church historian to become acquainted. . . . A pattern is a social institution or practice used to give content and intelligibility to otherwise unrealistic beliefs. What the axiom is in mathematics a pattern is in thought. . . . All Christian doctrines are patterns. They originate in the impulse to make something intelligible by discovering a likeness to something unquestioned.[1]

As he makes this approach to theology from the standpoint of social psychology, Dean Shailer Mathews draws a clear-cut distinction between the thought expressed and the pattern in which the thought is expressed. Theology represents man's attempt to communicate to others deep religious experiences. And the most dependable tools for this effort are those made in the images of established social patterns. We are safe in saying, then, that much of theology is relative and is bound by and limited to certain established and acceptable standards in man's social history. As man by research and insights moves into new areas

---

[1] Mathews, Shailer, "Doctrines As Social Patterns," *The Journal of Religion,* 10 (1930), pp. 4-9 *passim.*

of thought and passes beyond once acceptable patterns to other areas of life, he must seek new images in which to cast his vital thoughts. This is most significant in religion's attempt to gain the intellectual respect of the day and time in which it lives. Mathews continues:

> If religion is to have standing in the courts of today's intellect, it will have to find a pattern which is as axiomatic for modern man of our day as the pattern of sovereignty was to modern man of the sixteenth century. The doubts which rise from a distrust of a pattern cannot be laid by insistence upon that pattern.[2]

The great value then of theology is functional, and that function is to give as nearly as possible a rational statement of Christian experience, attitudes, and hopes. It is from this vantage point alone that theology can best be appreciated.

In a sense these social patterns represent the bottles, and the theological content represents the new wine. But one would be in grave error if he sought to identify the doctrine or the content with the social pattern or the container in which a doctrine is expressed in a given age of man's history. When these patterns have changed, or when the old bottles have grown too antiquated or too fragile to hold the content, one does not throw away the vital content with the changing or decaying form but seeks new current patterns in which the content can be placed. When the idea of God has grown too big to be housed in the social pattern of a feudal lord or a reigning king, men have found another suitable social pattern in which to express their idea of God. Hence the ever-changing form and systems of theology.

A careful study of the evolution of man's idea of God will reveal that from the standpoint of history the changes have not taken place in the nature of God Himself. They have taken place in man's formulation of the idea or—shall we say—in the shape of the containers in which these ideas were carried. When they

[2] *Ibid.*, pp. 12-13.

have discovered either by research, intuition, or revelation that an existing pattern could no longer justify the meaning of God, inquisitive minds have discarded these old containers and have sought others in which to pour the vital content.

Frequently the difference between orthodoxy and heterodoxy is in reality the difference in attitude towards the various social patterns, or forms by which the ideas are conveyed. In the history of the Christian religion many of the denominations with their peculiar emphases represent distinct containers. Since these differ widely, any attempt to reduce all of the denominational containers to the same shape or size would be hazardous. The great religious wars of history have been fought at the container level. Much blood has been shed in a vain attempt to force upon different people with their varied mental and emotional backgrounds a sameness in understanding that was not essential to theological clarity or to universal salvation. It is true that the content is regulated by the container as to form, shape, and appearance. If the container is square, the content will so appear. The shape of the content is a variable which is determined by the container and may be defined by the lines and limits of said container. But the quality of the content remains constant, assuming of course that the walls of the container are of such nature that the chemical reaction between the substance and the container will not produce an element that would change the content. Inasmuch as it is in the area of the content that there are great agreements among Christians the world over, it is on the content that we must concentrate.

An ecumenicity based on containers is not what we desire or what we should seek. It is an ecumenicity based on content that is most essential. We must always draw a distinction between substance, essence, or the basic things of religion and those forms or symbols by which the basic things are expressed. In this area, containers may be man-made, but the spiritual content is God-given. The vessel that contains the gospel truths may be earthen, but the gospel substance is a heavenly treasure. Paul, in writing to the Corinthians, seemed to be keenly aware of the difference between human capacity or talent, and the revealed word of God that man was asked to proclaim. Said he:

But we have this treasure in earthen vessels, that the excellency of the power may be of God, and not of us (2 Corinthians 4:7).

This great Apostle made it clear that the subject of the gospel they preached was not the earthen vessels but was Jesus Christ who had been revealed in them. And this divine light, fresh and searching from the mind of God, had been given unto them so that they could not boast about the message they proclaimed nor take pride in the riches of the content. They were, in a sense, the earthen vessels that had been blessed with a heavenly treasure.

In the Christian church we have too often fought battles over the things created by the human mind. We have too often sought to protect and render timeless the earthen vessels and have neglected the relevance of the heavenly treasure that passeth not away. Some have gone to the extreme of making an idol god out of the earthen vessels and have dealt with them as if they were eternal values. But time has taught us that that which is earthly is already doomed to death and will surely be turned to dust; its fleeting life shall be lost in the flux of things physical. Vessels will come and go, will change their forms with the passing ages, and be modified by the will of mankind, but the eternal content of the Christian religion will remain the same. The word of truth is the word of truth whether it be held by a homeless Abraham wandering from Ur of the Chaldees into the unknown places in the land of Canaan or proclaimed by the rustic prophet Amos, by the fiery-tongued Isaiah, or by the weeping prophet Jeremiah. The message of the kingdom is still the message of the kingdom whether proclaimed by John the Baptist, the humble preacher of the wilderness or by the barefooted preacher of Nazareth. The content of truth is the same whether preached by the Apostle Paul or proclaimed by the lonely preacher on the isle of Patmos. The gospel of Jesus Christ is just as eternal and just as mighty to save whether intoned by a priest before a candle-studded altar or a most eloquent preacher in a Protestant pulpit. The saving grace of Jesus Christ is just as powerful to cleanse, to redeem, and to sanctify whether preached or chanted among the learned of our metropolitan centers or humbly told from a country chapel by some rural saint crippled in language and maimed in speech.

The variable is the container, the wine skin, the earthen vessel. But the content is the heavenly treasure, the word of God. The container is like fading grass, but the content is the abiding and the eternal word of God. The prophet has so wisely said, "The grass withereth, the flowers fadeth: but the word of our God shall stand for ever" (Isaiah 40:8). Therefore we are sent to proclaim the gospel, not to protect it; to preach the word of truth with power, not to prove it; and to give the message of redemption freely to all men throughout the world, not to circumscribe it to any one nation, people, or clime. We must plant the seed of the gospel whatever the nature of the soil, knowing full well that in the process of germination the vital part of the seed shall burst its outer coat and leave its old container in the dust while it pushes its verdant head of new life up above the sod to breathe fresh air, to glow in the sun, to sway with healthy breezes, and finally to go through the progressive stages of fulfillment: first the blade, then the stalk, and then the grown fruit ready for the harvest time.

It is of the utmost importance that a container be adequate. The inference is, as we have already stated above, that there can be inadequate containers. Great paintings must be placed upon the canvas that is sufficient to hold them through the years; for if the canvas fails, the beauty of the painting will be damaged with the canvas. No container is adequate for spiritual content that cannot support, at least for a season, the quality of the content. In the science laboratory one must be sure to find the right container for various substances. Containers that may hold water may not be able to contain liquid gas. Containers that are sufficient for water may not hold fermenting wine. What is true in science is true in religion; the container must be adequate to hold the spiritual content. Jesus had this in mind when He spoke the parable to which we referred above. We must not put new wine into inadequate bottles lest the inadequate bottle should break and the wine be lost. A container that is not adequate for the content will destroy both itself and the content.

A theological concept that is outmoded by the facts of science or the findings of philosophy or the testimony of advancing life cannot be employed in the service of moral and spiritual truths. A theological concept that was restricted to the narrow ritualism of the ancient Hebrews was inadequate to contain the universal message of the Christian religion. This was one of the early battles that Paul fought with the Judaizing teachers within the churches of his day. Some insisted on circumcision as the test of a believer's standing with Jesus Christ and the church. It was the verdict of Paul that though adequate for the Hebrew concept of religion, this was too narrow for a religion that was to include "THE WHOSOEVER WILL" of Jesus Chirst whose limits include all the world.

Containers or patterns are valuable, but they are not the most important things in the field of Christian experience. We must not concentrate all of our efforts on selecting adequate containers, giving our energies to beautifying and embellishing the same at the expense of the right content. There is the danger of becoming so devoted to the problem of adjusting past religious experiences to the intellectual climate of the day that we might overlook the need for a continuing vital religious experience itself. We may worship the form and miss the religious forces. We may lose ourselves in the art of the physical structure of the cathedral and neglect the Christ who is the legitimate inspiration of the cathedral. When devotion to the expressions of religion develop to the point that religion fades into mere externalism, then the church has fallen upon evil days, and the hour for a new searching of heart has come. It was against such externalism in religion that Jesus spoke with such biting criticism of the ancient Pharisees. He said unto them:

> Woe unto you, scribes and Pharisees, hypocrites! for ye make clean the outside of the cup and of the platter, but within they are full of exhortation and excess. Thou blind Pharisee, cleanse first that which is within the cup and platter, that the outside of them may be clean also. Woe unto you, scribes and Pharisees, hypocrites! For ye are likened to whited sepulchres which indeed appear beautiful outward, but are within full of dead men's bones, and of all uncleanness (St. Matthew 23:25-27).

However important they might be, containers can never be a substitute for vital content. Let the most skilled minds do their best work in shaping containers and in rendering their workmanship almost perfect, and let the work of art add thereto its noble charms and rare beauty; but if the content is diluted or lacking in reality, the container can serve little purpose. Scholars and religious leaders may labor incessantly to recreate the outer forms of religion and seek to build a united body, but all is vain unless the content retains its creative and redemptive value. Embellished containers may attract attention for a season; but when thirsty souls approach them and find the content is not there, the containers lose their attraction and the weary souls seek life from other sources.

It is possible to lose our minds in externals and in what seems to be reality and therby miss completely the divine content of saving grace. Devotion to externals in religion may cause men to miss the substance of all of God's spiritual gifts. Jesus told the Pharisees it was all right to make the outside of the cup clean, but in reality the outside could be only partially clean unless the inside were clean also. The clean platters exist as containers for the pure substance; if the substance is missing, even clean platters will not suffice.

How fine it is for scholars to work overtime in an attempt to render theological concepts intellectually respectable. But this is not enough. The inside of religion, the soul of it, must be kept pure and creative. And if scholarship does refine the ideas, and theology renders all the notions most attractive from the outside, the life of the believer and that of the whole church may be just as poverty-stricken as the Pharisees to whom Jesus spoke.

In this age of great concern for Christian unity there is a temptation to hasten to the formulation of externals on which Christians may quickly agree. But it is much better to be re-tarded in our agreements of externals and re-vitalize the inner life of the spirit. When the fellowship between Christians was broken in the past and misunderstanding crept in as strife, hatred, and prejudice gripped the hearts of the professed be-lievers, it was much better for them to separate into different groups. After separation it was possible to establish some rapport between the various bodies which would have been impossible if there had continued a running battle across the years, building up animosities and nullifying the purpose of the Kingdom of God. While it is regrettable that divisions have crept into the Christian ranks, it is my conviction that these divisions reveal to us how weak the inner content was and how depleted was the practical love of Christ between us. As we have lived in our respective frameworks as denominations, we have had a chance to know repentance, to discover, and to de-velop a Christian vitality that should now be strong enough to lead us into the selection of forms by which the vitality of Christian life may be expressed.

Furthermore, if containers were perfect and the content held therein were also perfect, the content still represents only a very small part of the total spiritual content. This is true in every denomination and every group of believers both collectively and individually. If and when all theological systems are per-fected and the inspired life of the Spirit of God has filled every human heart to overflowing, there will still be a vast area of unknown spiritual truths, undiscovered parts of the Divine Plan. As Paul once said, at best we know in part and we prophesy in part. It seems that the Fourth Gospel refers to this vast area of life that Jesus proclaimed when its author says:

And there are also many other things which Jesus did, the which, if they should be written every one, I suppose that even the world itself could not contain the books that should be written (St. John 21:25).

Who then should boast of the content of his theology or of the measure of his doctrine? And what church should lay claim to finality in the matter of what she knows and proclaims about the revelation of Jesus Christ? What if a container is filled to the brim with undisputed divine truth? Can one say that his container has exhausted all of the content of divine revelation and that his mind has completely tapped all of the resources of the Divine Mind?

One container is not big enough to exhaust the fullness of Jesus Christ or to hold all the mysteries of Divine Grace. In order to exhaust the resources of the gospel of Jesus Christ, there must be more and larger containers than are reflected in the minds of men. And if there were more containers there would be the need for more worlds to hold the containers of so great a salvation. But why lose ourselves in speculation in our attempt to grasp the measure of God's boundless love and limitless grace? Let us take counsel from the fruitless quest of Job and confess that the problem is beyond our reach; let us not grow weary with seeking what the mind can never find. What Job said more than three thousand years ago is still true and will be up-to-date millions of years from now.

Canst thou by searching find out God? Canst thou find out the Almighty unto perfection? It is as high as heaven; what canst thou do? Deeper than hell; what canst thou know? The measure thereof is longer than the earth, and broader than the sea (Job 11:7-9).

In the light of the limitations of our capacities we may well work for the Kingdom of God without pride or prejudice, holding no brief for the claims of others, for all are restricted by the incompleteness of the knowledge they possess. No man knows enough about the Kingdom of God to be justified in seeking to close the doors in the face of any other because of what he does not know. And no church is pure enough to lock its doors of grace against any repentant sinner or any seeking and weary believer. Let us accept our limitations with faith and go forth to use our gifts with hope as we labor with others for the Kingdom that is and that is sure to come.

In view of our discussion in this chapter, we are now ready to deal more specifically with the content of our Christian faith on which there is great agreement among all believers, and all denominations of Christians in the world. For if the content be known and grasped, the soul of man will burst forth from the fetters of the past and find a form for its expression. All believers have long since agreed on this spiritual content. These are the things without which there could be no church, no ministry of Jesus Christ, and no fellowship of the spirit. It is true that the spiritual content of the Christian Church represents many and varied elements. Time and space would not permit our dealing with all of them in this connection; we shall limit ourselves to four of the basic things on which Christians have long since agreed: God as Creator, Preserver, and Savior of Mankind; The Miracle of Jesus Christ; The Unique Function of the Holy Spirit; and the Christian Concept of Man.

II

SOME BASIC CHRISTIAN AGREEMENTS

5

GOD AS CREATOR, PRESERVER AND SAVIOR OF MANKIND

THE VARIED IDEAS OF GOD, and the expressions of the human mind's understanding of the revelation of God, are shaped according to the *intelligence tendencies* of those who wrestle with these themes. The philosophical mind rejects all aspects of God that cannot be justified by the canons of reason or sustained by the most thorough investigation. In the scientific approach to religion, one observes many of the old concepts being swept away; as a result, a generation of doubters has emerged who refuse to accept the faith of their fathers because in their judgment such a faith does not harmonize with the science of the day.

The average man who goes about his work from day to day, busy with the tasks of earning a livelihood and of seeking workable solutions to the problems that he faces, is not primarily concerned with adjusting his idea of God to the intellectual climate in which he lives. He is more concerned with the problem of finding a firm rock on which to stand amidst the flow and flux of human life. This average mind has made itself satisfied with the affirmation of saints in ages past by accepting as true the existing catalog of their experiences with God and by believing the testimony of those who have by faith seen the Lord of life and who have through dedication known of His presence and power.

There runs through all the varied experiences and ideas of God some unchanging and abiding elements, some acceptable threads of truth that cannot be doubted or denied. The first of these is that God is life. Whenever Christians cite the name of God they speak of LIFE at its best. Even when minds tutored in modern philosophy and shaped by the discipline of science come to accept any kind of god, life is one of the basic ideas underlying their concept of god. Since our God is not a God of the dead but a God of the living, our God is not death, but life.

On this point the writer of the Book of Genesis agrees with the most gifted theologian of the twentieth century. Any Christian thought that has been influenced by a process philosophy and the evolutionary concept of life is as much life-centered in its doctrine of God as is the view of orthodox theologians who talk of God as the great absolute by whose power all things are created. Here theistic naturalism joins with the theism of orthodox theology because they share a common belief in life. While the manner of expression may differ between God the creator as seen by an ancient Hebrew thinker and God the principle of concretion as observed by Alfred North Whitehead and Henry Nelson Wieman, God as life is an undisputed and accepted fact in each system of thought. In the one case He speaks and it is done; He commands and it stands fast. In the case of the other He moves amidst the matter of nature as a force of creativity, bringing a dead order to life and infusing new energy in a created order that would otherwise slowly move to decay and death.

When we say God is life we are aware that life itself is a mystery, and a complete definition of it escapes our grasp, but the following things may be said of it. First, life is self-sustaining. Wherever there is a living order there is a being that has the power, at least in part, to sustain itself by its own efforts. Although living plants draw their sustenance from the elements, they must somehow turn those elements into foods that will keep them. By their roots they seek and receive the ready nourishment from the soil; by their leaves and branches they take in the benediction of light, heat and food from the refreshing breeze. What is said of plants may increasingly be said of lower animals and even of men. They must have the power to sustain themselves through their efforts, that is, to use their environments in such a way that their systems will know life. But these imperfect illustrations do not give us the whole lesson that we seek, for all living things are most dependent upon the things in the world about them, and their natures not only are marked for decay but also are slowly moving toward the silent chambers of death.

When we apply the statement to God, that is, that He is self-sustaining, we mean that He exists by the power of His own being and relies not on that *which was* or that *which is*, or that *which is yet to come*. When the "old theologians" mentioned "free" as an attribute of God, they were trying to convey the idea that He lived and moved by the power of His own being and did not await the will of any other power to realize the fullness of His own selfhood.

Furthermore, it is the nature of life to produce life. Life possesses the urge and the power to create. The higher the plane of life, the greater and more comprehensible is the power to create. In the Book of Genesis, God goes about the task of making the earth and the heavens. He sows seeds in the earth, peoples the plains with animals, sets the stars, and then divides day and night by the moving splendor of the moon and the sun. Finally, out of the dust of the earth He forms man and makes him into His own image. Whatever else is said of the author of the Book of Genesis, one must agree that he states the fact about God that the wisdom of all ages has not reversed, and the thinkers throughout history have not refuted: God is the giver of life.

The writer of the Fourth Gospel has profited by the revelation of centuries and by the testimony of history, and yet when he begins the story of his great gospel, he begins where the author of the Book of Genesis begins. In four brief verses he compresses the story of three long chapters in the Book of Genesis and tells what happened in the span of seven days. Said he:

In the beginning was the Word, and the Word was with God and the Word was God. The same was in the beginning with God. All things were made by him; and without him was not any thing made that was made. In him was life; and the life was the light of men (St. John 1:1-4).

The writer of the Fourth Gospel gives the reason for this broad creative act in one word: LIFE. Because of the LIFE in Him the great God gave LIFE to the universe. Because of the LIFE from Him men possessed the light of wisdom and the light of the Spirit. It is this shining light in men that enables them to see, though imperfectly, some of the acts of divine wisdom. The Christian church is agreed that the meaning of our universe may be determined from the fact that God is life. When we think of Him as the energizing power in our whole cosmic structure, we can rest on the fact that God is life. This unquestioned agreement has remained throughout history in the Christian church.

God is the source of all life. The creative acts through which He brought worlds into being may be traced not only to the spoken word but also to the nature of God Himself. In Him resided life, and the out-flowing of this life resulted in what we call creation. It is not unreasonable to assume that, in some form, acts of creation are still going on because life still flows from God as the fountainhead of LIFE. Jesus seemed to have recognized this when He said: "My Father worketh hitherto and I work." Students of process philosophy are not too far removed from that theistic position which recognizes the continuous flow of life from God. He is the giver of all life, and from Him all creative gifts come forth. But unlike process philosophy, here God is the spring from which the bounties come and by His guidance and providence, this stream of values flows through the whole field of time, cutting valleys through the rocks of human resistance and making oases in the deserts of human depravity.

But God is not only a source of life in the ordinary sense of the word; He is also the source of the higher order of life that includes not only the natural and the animal order of existence but also the best in human nature. When he condemned the Athenians for their worship of idol gods, Paul hastened to correct their error by pointing them to the eternal God who was the creator of all men and of all nations. This God whom Paul introduces was the one who gave life and breath to all.

. . . and hath made of one blood all nations of men for to dwell on all the face of the earth, and hath determined the times before appointed, and the bounds of their habitation. . . . For in him we live, and move, and have our being; as certain also of your own poets have said, For we are also His offsprings (Acts 17:26-28).

Here God becomes the source of being, that is, the source of existence, the source of human personality. This fact, thought Paul, was enough to correct the sins of idolatry and to put to naught the representation of the God-head by gold, silver, or stone or anything graven by man's device. Christians have agreed that if we would understand man at his best we must not look down to the slime of the earth or to the scum of some distant sea, nor should we gaze upon the habitations of ancient caves and bosky dens. We must look upward toward the heights and behold the God of history and the God of Jesus Christ in and through whom human life has come into existence.

As we approach the God of life and feel the impact of His personality and listen to His voice, we discover our unique kinship with our Creator. The life in man, though feeble, feels a kinship with abundant life in God and looks toward Him and calls Him Father. But this discovery is not the exclusive result of man's effort. It is largely due to what God has given to man. The revelation of Himself as a God who cares and provides has impressed the conscience of mankind with the image of God as Father. Believers who understand the tender concern of the living God do not find it difficult to live a life of prayer. A God of unfolding life, as a principle of concretion, or God as a powerful creator interested only in the making of worlds, does not and cannot inspire Christian prayer. God is more than a cosmic mechanic engaged in arranging, shaping, and repairing the universe. He is more than a master geologist concerned with the making and adjusting of stones and massive rocks. God is more than the energy of atoms and the heat and fire of the molecules of the earth. *God is Father.*

God has shown His Fatherhood in a measure by feeding the fowls of the air who know not to sow seeds in the spring or to reap harvest from autumn fields. They do not store up grain in barns nor plan their budgets for the coming seasons; yet they are somehow fed out of the storehouse of nature and the abundant offerings of fruitful fields. The divine concern for beauty and grace is reflected in the flowers of the field, the spotless robes that lilies wear. Yet these beautiful specimens of nature do not toil at a given task nor do they weave the garments they possess. Flowers and vegetations are short-lived but are designed with rare distinction and draped with gorgeous beauty.

These expressions of God's concern are preliminary steps, for the Fatherhood of God is not fully revealed here. We must reflect on what He does for the mankind that He has made in His image and equipped to seek His fullness. God wants us to knock at the door of hope and stand before His smiling face and ask of Him the things that body and soul desire. Without this keen awareness of God's concern for His people, Christian prayer might well be reduced to an unwise leap in the dark, auto-suggestion, self-torture or self-deception.

Because God is our Father, Jesus taught that we should guard against such heathen practices as the vain use of words or the employment of charms and symbols to placate some angry and heartless spirits. Jesus revealed that the man who speaks to God speaks to his Father who knows and cares. It is not man's asking that puts God in an attitude of tender care. His nature and His life have already rendered Him so. Therefore Jesus taught that when we pray, we must begin with the statement of fact, faith, and warmth of relation which reflects our kinship with the God to whom we pray: "Our Father which art in heaven."

What if we believers are caught in a chain of circumstances in which we are pelted by the fiery darts of the wicked one? What if the filth of a world of slums has marred our faces and spoiled the God-given image within? What if through ignorance and weakness we have drifted into some poverty-stricken land where sin is might and death is king? What if we are tempted to fear and dread amidst the howls of the storms of corruption and the earth-shaking thunders of decay? And what if the skies of our experiences are overcast with deep, dark clouds trembling with despair and threatening diseaser? In spite of all of these there is no gulf separating us children of the lowly earth from the Father of the vaulted skies. Jesus has taught well that when we pray we may say "Our Father" for He is there and He is also here. He is high in the heavens above but also in reach of the cries, needs and sorrows of the earth. God, the source of LIFE, is also the Father of LIFE.

Not only is God LIFE; He is also LOVE. It is quite essential for man to know this aspect of God because the story of man is one of pride, disobedience, sin, guilt, condemnation, and death. He has not been as thankful to God as he should have been for all the blessings of life that he has received. As a prodigal he has drifted from his Father's house, has journeyed to strange lands, and does not of himself deserve the right to live in his Father's house. Because of his transgressions, man has been considered as an alien and a stranger to the God who made him and to the Father who provides for him. According to the laws of Moses, the wrath of God resulted from man's rebellion. The story of the approach to Mount Sinai, The Mount of God, dramatizes the anger of God against sinful men.

Shortly after the children of Israel had gone out of the land

of Egypt into the wilderness toward the land of Canaan, the
Lord told Moses to prepare the people:

And the Lord said unto Moses, go unto the people, and sanctify
them today and tomorrow, and let them wash their clothes, and be
ready against the third day: for the third day the Lord will come
down in the sight of all the people upon Mount Sinai. And thou shall
set bounds unto the people round about, saying, Take heed to yourselves, that ye go not up into the mount, or touch the border of it:
whosoever touches the mount shall be surely put to death: There shall
not an hand touch it, but he shall surely be stoned, or shot through;
whether it be beast or man, it shall not live . . . (Exodus 19:10-13).

God appears exclusive and apart. His presence repels, and His
private habitation could not be touched by unworthy men.

When He did come on the third day, He came in sternness
and in the expressions of terror and dread. The angry elements
and the frowning heavens represented His presence.

And it came to pass on the third day in the morning, that there were
thunders and lightnings, and a thick cloud upon the mount, and the
voice of the trumpet exceedingly loud; so that all the people that was
in the camp trembled. And Moses brought forth the people out of the
camp to meet with God; and they stood at the nether part of the
mount. And Mount Sinai was altogether on a smoke, because the Lord
descended upon it in fire: and the smoke thereof ascended as the
smoke of a furnace, and the whole mount quaked greatly (Exodus
19:16-18).

The approach of God excited fear, and the people were warned
to stay their distance. God's presence was marked by cataclysms
of nature: the trembling and quaking of the mountain, the noise
and fiery voice of thunder.

But such is not the Christian view of God. Christians main-
tain that God is kind and gentle, full of compassion, the very
personification of LOVE. Thus He is more than a Father who

cares for and loves His creatures; He himself is LOVE. He possesses such a nature that He is not motivated by merit as He faces men with their needs and their sins. He does not delay His coming. He does not require a period of three days or three months or three years of cleansing before man can come close to His presence. Every hour is God's hour, and every moment of time is the accepted time for God to meet and deal with His unworthy children. His acts of redemption are motivated by His ability to treat the unworthy as though they were worthy.

God does not need to strive with Himself in order to show mercy to sinners or to crown the undeserving with divine merit. There is no war within His being between justice and love. All the judicial qualities of His nature are merged in the one dominating fact of His being, and that is the fact of love. He need not labor to be kind to the unkind or to extend a hand of clemency to the wretched because HE IS LOVE. He is so constituted in His nature that He can extend himself to the undeserving without in any way taxing the harmony of His being. How this is done is beyond us. In fact, how to explain the harmony of justice, righteousness, love, and mercy is not the task to which the average believer need address himself. These are indeed mysteries which merit thought and meditation, but for our purposes we rest our souls by faith in the fact that our God is a God of love.

We are not unmindful of the problem of evil and suffering that is abroad in the world. However, we are not concerned here about trying to reduce the acts of God to the level of human comprehension; nor do we elect to embark upon a speculative journey by which we would demand of eternity that it gauge all of its long-range plans by the limits of the fleeting moments of time. It is enough for us to embrace by faith the fact that the Lord of our lives and the Master of the universe is a God of love.

From this faith comes encouragement, solace, comfort, and joy. For we know that our world is not left totally in the hands of the evil one, and we shall not remain the helpless victims of sin and Satan. In this faith and consciousness that our God is a God of love we go forward amidst the shadows, encouraged by a light that shines in darkness because the darkness has not put it out. We journey on with hope and confidence; in the chill of threatening despair we feel the warmth of His everlasting presence. God is love is the fact on which sinful man may build his hopes and is the eternal rock of salvation on which the weary may stand without fear and trembling. We are not able to know completely the nature of love and therefore have not the power to adequately analyze the term. But there are some bits of historical information that will help us to say at least faintly what we mean when we say God is love.

The first of these recorded experiences may be taken from the everyday records of human existence and is demonstrated by the affection and devotion of a mother to her child. Here one sees a quality of life that gives itself and never expects or demands a full reward in return. Here is an example of a quality of life that suffers without complaining and attaches itself to its object without shame or fear, and every interest present in this relationship is focused on the completion and fulfillment of life. A more exhaustive study of the mother's love will give us faint glimpses into the greatness of the statement that God is love.

A second illustration of the loftiness of the thought of love is seen in Paul's psalm of love in Chapter 13 of his first letter to the Corinthians. When one reads this passage with care, he is moved to a greater appreciation of the meaning of love. Love has the quality to suffer and yet not retreat from deeds of mercy and acts of kindness. Love carries with it no envy. When it is sinned against, it sins not. When it has rendered the greatest deeds of charity and has extended the most patient and forgiving hands to offending powers, love still refuses to vaunt itself, does not feed on pride or the lust of power, and is never puffed up. In its thoughts no evil comes no matter how sinful or evil the circumstances in which it lives. In the presence of insults and provocations love is not easily moved or quickly provoked. The quest of love is not for itself. The quest of love is its object, though unworthy, undeserving, and sinful. Love has the keenest respect for truth and does not seek to evade the facts however grim but throws its radiant light over the grimmest facts and purges that which is impure until the unclean comes forth clear as the dawn and pure as the sun. Love bears all things in spite of the wretchedness of the burdens. Love stands firm and carries its share.

Paul reveals that love is something that never fails, and he catalogs a number of forces, principles, and powers but sees in all of these, however, great indications of future failures. Some of the great Christian virtues will come to their journey's end because the time will come when their functions will have no meaning and their mission no purpose. When the journey of the Christian life is finished, we will no longer need the shining torch of faith. When weary souls have seized the anticipated things and have come at last into the Canaan of all of the promised blessings of eternal life, then the work of hope will be done and its place no longer needed. But since love is best exercised in relationships and since it is God, then it goes on and on throughout the joyous bliss of all eternity. Paul quickens the imagination in this passage on love and gives us profound ideas as to some of the great qualities that are brought into focus when we say that God is love.

Still another indication of the quality of love in God is the whole mission of Jesus Christ which was enveloped in the spirit of love. The writer of the Fourth Gospel explains the mission of Jesus in terms of His Father's love. Jesus came into the world as a gift from God to the humble men and women who were lost and needed salvation. This transaction was a great mystery, a mystery that the writer of the Fourth Gospel could not explain and labored not to analyze. He found his only answer in the fact of the love of God. Said he: "For God so loved the world, that He gave His only begotten Son, that whosoever believeth in Him should not perish, but have everlasting life" (John 3:16). There is no measure of this love. The writer simply says: "GOD SO LOVED . . ."

The writer of First John sees that human beings have been made sons of God by a manner of love that God bestowed. Says he: "Behold, what manner of love the Father hath bestowed upon us, that we should be called the sons of God . . ." (I John 3:1). Jesus was not only given in love and through love, but in His own life and character reveals the nature and the quality of the love that was God! The story of His life is a story of humility, service and sacrifice. Never at any time did He contend for rank for Himself. Never at any moment did He turn from the most humble in order to remain detached from the needs and woes of human life. He was concerned about the hungry and fed them. He was touched by the depth of human sorrow and wept with those who grieved. He sought the lost for their salvation when spurned and cursed by them. He gave the utmost of Himself that the riches of the divine image might be restored to the poor in spirit and the humble in heart. The life, mission, and character of Jesus Christ is a concrete example of the nature and meaning of the love of God.

The ideas of God as expressed here are simple yet profound enough to claim the agreement of all believers. These concepts tend to unite the hearts and minds of men from all nations and to lift every denomination of Christians into an undisputed fellowship that the things of the world cannot negate and the evils of men need not destroy.

One need not wonder about who God is and what God is when one says of Him: GOD IS LOVE, for the character of Jesus reveals Him. The personality of Jesus reflects the quality of the Divine Life, and His message to the humble and to the weak reassures all men of the reality and the inclusiveness of the LOVE of God.

THE MIRACLE OF JESUS CHRIST

WHEN WE BEHOLD the personality and the message of Jesus, we are impressed and moved to deep thought and meditation. He stands firmly in spite of the moving tide of ages. Jesus is today what He was yesterday and bids fair to be tomorrow what He is today. His message has attracted people from all stations of life. The finger of history has pointed at Him; He has been catalogued among the leading spirits of mankind. The best in the prophetic history of the Hebrews was orientated towards the quality of life dramatized in Jesus Christ. It matters not whether the ideal of the Hebrew prophets was a personality moving down the highway of time as a promised Messiah or whether this ideal person was a small community dedicated to the service and will of God. In each case, the life of Jesus and His community message to both small and great seemed to have fulfilled the highest expectations of the Hebrews.

Those who have not elected to follow Him have looked on Him in wonderment. When they could not fully understand His motives and manner of living, they have exclaimed: "Behold the Man" whose purpose is unique, whose message is profound, and whose vision escapes human comprehension. Some have looked on Him as a miracle worker whose power came from above and whose authority was given by God. They said of Him in the day of His early ministry and they have testified the same in subsequent history: "No man can do the miracle that He doeth except God be with Him." Still other sensitive souls have been so impressed with this STRANGE MAN of history that

59

they have put aside their doubts, saying of Him: "Surely this Man is the Son of God." Hardened politicians who were bent on condemning Him by finding some reason for His capture and arrest, upon hearing Him speak have returned to those higher in authority and reported to them: We did not capture the man. We found no reason to arrest him and we felt unworthy to approach him. His actions were peculiar, His message seemed strange, and His speech was without comparison. "Never man spake like this man" (St. John 7:46).

The Christian church has attached a holy significance to Jesus Christ and has considered Him the author and the finisher of her redemption, the captain of her salvation, the living bread for her hungry souls, and the water of life that is constantly overflowing within her as an eternal spring. He is to the church the peculiar reason for her existence and the eternal foundation on which she stands. With Edward Mote the church has been singing through the ages:

> My hope is built on nothing less
> Than Jesus' blood and righteousness;
> I dare not trust the sweetest frame,
> But wholly lean on Jesus' name:
>
> When darkness veils His lovely face,
> I rest on His unchanging grace;
> In every high and stormy gale,
> My anchor holds within the veil:
>
> His oath, His covenant and blood,
> Support me in the whelming flood:
> When all around my soul gives way,
> He then is all my hope and stay:
>
> On Christ, the solid Rock, I stand,
> All other ground is sinking sand,
> All other ground is sinking sand.

Thus Jesus, the man of mystery and the miracle of history, still moves the world to wonder and impells believers to faith and repentance.

What is this miracle of Jesus? What is the mystery of His character, the force and power of His personality? And why the grandeur that Christian history has ascribed to Him? These questions are raised in an attempt to further emphasize the uniqueness of the Son of God, knowing full well that any answers given will be only fragmentary. For although we look and live by faith, we can grasp but little and understand but vaguely. We really do see as through a glass darkly and know only in part the mystery of so great a spirit. It is not too strange that our prophecy shall be partial; we approach a peculiar task poorly equipped to perform it well.

In our telling of the might of so holy a being, we are fully aware that our powers have been dulled by centuries of ignorance and their strength weakened by ages of sin. But faith urges us to speak of the divine truth in Jesus Christ, though we stammer and stutter because of tongues unskilled in speech and lips only partly purged by the cleansing fires of the Holy Spirit.

Speak we must, for silence would be less golden than utterance, and indifference would feed the already swollen streams of doubt; to hold our peace would encourage a war among the rocks and a strange testimony in the realms of nature. Paul heard in the bosom of the earth a voice of discontent and a shout of uneasy grief and protest, as if there was a profound dissatisfaction and a patience that was growing weary in the waiting for the manifestation of the will of God among the sons of men. Speaking of the ones who praised Him, Jesus Himself once said: "If these should hold their peace the stones would immediately cry out" (St. Luke 19:40). The church therefore is compelled to give her testimony of Jesus Christ.

We first discover the miracle of Jesus in His moral mastery of life. He was a man in whose mouth there was no guile and in whose heart sin found no place. Even His enemies never pro-

duced any trustworthy evidence against Him. When they sought
to condemn Him through false witnesses, they found none whose
testimony established a defective character. Even when Judas
accepted thirty pieces of silver to betray Him, all he could do
was lead the mob out to the garden spot where Jesus so often
went to pray.

To say that Jesus was a man who knew no sin may be considered a negative approach. But when we realize how afflicted
mankind is with sin, it is but natural that the human mind would
be awe-stricken by the vision of a man who knew no sin and in
whose mouth no guile was ever found. Some of the apostles
were moved to write of this aspect. Said the writer of the Book
of Hebrews: "For we have not an high priest which cannot be
touched with the feeling of our infirmities, but was in all points
tempted like as we are, yet without sin" (4:15). For sinful creatures this is a miraculous sight to behold, and such creatures
gaze in awe upon the mystery and the greatness of the man
Christ Jesus. For those who are so frequently defeated in their
moral efforts to follow the light of the "oughtness" of conscience,
the sinless life of Jesus will always be a miracle. What a privilege
for the weak and the imperfect! What an inspiration for those
who are tempted to surrender and yield the mastery of life to
the forces of sin! In the presence of the man Christ Jesus one
cannot conclude that all human creatures are helpless pawns in
the hands of the daemonic powers of the universe. Here is a
conqueror who has never bowed His knees under the sway of
Baal, stooped to the lust of power, nor worshipped the god of
greed. Here is a refreshing spring in the desert of human life
and a city of refuge for those who seek the highest values of
life.

On the more positive side, Jesus endured the privations of
human life, the insults of men, and the temptation of the evil
one but still radiated a spiritual power. None of His time was
given to avenging His hurts or to punishing His enemies. His
was a life dedicated to the mystery of love and to the service of

all mankind. As the revelation of a God of love, He was Love in action. He was Love walking the streets of towns and villages, going about the countrysides in fields and in homes. He was Love on a mission of doing good.

He had the power to crush His enemies, but as a force of Love He lived above and beyond the threat and the use of physical forces. The community that He came to establish did not require a sword and did not need the services of any standing armies of destruction or of any power to bring death to those who loved Him not. Said He: "I came not to destroy but to fulfill." He came proclaiming the ideal in order to make it real. He embodied the visions of prophets of justice and peace in order to bring them into the common practice of man. He identified the victor of the sword with the victim of it. To Him there could be no peace through war, no brotherhood born in the throes of blood-stained battlefields; no moral and spiritual help could come through the practice of hate or through the deeds of slaughter. No salvation could ever come by seeking the will of man in contrast to the will of God. Jesus knew by the power of spiritual insights what it has taken the nations of the modern world centuries to learn and what western civilization has at long last discovered after the pain, the carnage, destruction, and deaths of two world wars. Jesus knew the results of envy, prejudice, hatred and conflict. He knew this without reading it from the grim spectre of battlefields or learning it from the woes of the bereaved, the groans of the dying, and the mangled forms of the dead.

He took delight in lifting burdens from the hearts of the needy. He came to save those who were lost. This was no mere professional performance; rather, it was deep in the soul of the man. He was bound to the people of the world by ties of affection and wedded to all by the power of love. And He proclaimed His visions of love as a way of life and as the hope of all mankind. Through love, Jesus releases a new moral force in the world and the world has not been able to destroy it.

Many symbols and parables have been employed in man's attempt to relate the miracle of Jesus. In this attempt, the resources of the ages have been tapped, and the best talents in science, philosophy, art, music, and literature have been summoned. These efforts have not been wholly in vain, for they have left their marks on the pages of history; their labors still bear the golden fruits of inspiration. If there were no other rewards of record, the creative influence that this great personality has had in all the areas of life would pay the humble seekers for their efforts. A great religious thinker about fifty years ago set forth his impression of Jesus in the following words:

Let us, then, stand unwaveringly by this fresh impression of reality. Unhampered by any theology and philosophy whatsoever, let us stick to what we see. The riddle of this man shall remain a riddle for us— it shall not with our consent be deprived of its immediate fascination and its immediate effect by the development of a doctrine. Here is a humanity which is diaphanous to the Spirit and to God. Here or nowhere we may catch a presentiment of what happens when God finds full entrance into human actuality and man finds full entrance into divine truth. Here or nowhere we feel is the prime example of how Divine Being can stream through a human being, how a human being may be set aglow by the Divine.[1]

Jesus Christ has enriched every area of human life, and the most constructive agencies of the human mind have labored hard to set forth the mystery of Jesus in true prospect. But when every human mind has done its best there still stands before the world the unknown, incomprehensible, and abiding quality of the life of Jesus Christ.

The Christian church accepts the miracle of Jesus as the basic tenet of her faith. There is no Christian church where the personality of Jesus is left out. He is to the Christian believer the Great Wonder of the World, although historians have looked

[1] Friedrich Rittelmeyer, *Behold The Man* (New York, Macmillan, 1929), pp. 89-90.

upon the works of human hands and the artifices of nature in order to select what they delight to call The Seven Wonders of the World.

Our Christian faith has given us a living, God-revealing personality of history—Jesus, the Christ. Psychology has granted us no common norm with which to measure Him. Sociology gives us no trustworthy standards by which His life may be determined. His mystery rests not in His genealogy: the rich fruit of His being cannot be traced from His family tree. His social milieu gives no adequate cue to the reason for His manner of life because Nazareth, His home, was not famed for producing great men; no distinguished, flaming prophet of history had come out of the city. In fact, in the day of Jesus, the accepted conclusion was that "no good thing could come out of Nazareth."

To be true to the facts, we must admit that Jesus had a worthy religious background. He was in some instances a direct spiritual descendant of that worthy line of Hebrew prophets who put righteousness before ritual, justice before religious and natural jurisprudence. Theirs was not merely a God of smoking altars, lifeless ceremonies, One who could be satisfied with offerings of gold and silver, and the sacrifice of fowls or the creeping things of the earth. These prophets revealed a God who hated meaningless sacrifices and who demanded that justice should roll down like waters and that righteousness should flow as a mighty stream. To say that Jesus was not a part of the great prophetic tradition of the ancient Hebrew people represents disloyalty to the facts as we know them and a denial of the voice of history as it speaks.

But when we have given history full credit for all the good that it has done for Jesus and properly assessed all the legacies from the past that fed the life-stream of His religion, we must still admit that there were elements in the life of Jesus that transcended the claims of history and rose above the limitations of geography and of time. We must proclaim and agree that the life of Jesus was a Miracle.

Yet when the church attempts to explain the Miracle of Jesus, points of disagreement appear. The church is as divided and as different as are the mental outlooks, dispositions, and attitudes of the believers who comprise it. Some have sought to explain the miracle of Jesus by beginning with the nature of His birth. For them, the virgin birth is the basis for the origin, character, mission, and destiny of God's Holy Child. It was by special divine intervention that the Heavenly Child was brought forth. The occasion of the birth was attended by the appearance of strange meteors and by the commission and the movement of a new star while angels hallowed the sacred hour with glorious music, praising God and proclaiming to the inhabitants of the earth that Divine Promise was fulfilled: the expected Messiah had come, and a new reign of God began for the redemption of the lost sons of men.

When the music is reduced to a message, the star is accepted as a sign, the words spoken to the shepherds as the voice of God, and the beauty of the scene interpreted as the boldness of God to seek and to save the lost, then we know that the artful presentation of the event is man's effort to explain the true meaning of the miracle of Jesus Christ. For the gospel writers of the books of Matthew and Luke knew full well that the holy life of Jesus could not be fully explained by the law of human procreation. A guiltless child could not come from the sinful nature of Adam's clan, and the Messiah of God could never be contained within the limits of the urges of human reproduction; hence, they found their answer to the miracle in the divine origin of the conception and the heavenly scene attending the holy birth.

Needless to say, there are wide differences on the meaning, manner, and nature of the virgin birth. Heated theological battles have been waged over it, the minds of medical men have moved to revolt, skeptics have found food to satiate their appetites, and philosophers with their instruments of realism have sought to remove this story as an unnecessary appendage from the sacred records of old. Some have tried to explain the miracle of Jesus by the sudden blast of the Eternal and by the clear voice of God which broke the news in His soul that He was different, called of God, the Messiah, endowed with the Holy Spirit for the purpose of healing the broken in heart, giving sight to the blind, setting at liberty those who are bruised, preaching the acceptable year of the Lord, and redeeming the lost from ruin and death.

Others, like the writer of the Fourth Gospel, find only one answer to the miracle of Jesus, not in history or in time, but in the plan of God as revealed in eternity. Such a being had His beginning with His father and was present in the acts of creation. For the Scripture says: "In the beginning was the Word, and the Word was with God, and the Word was God. The same was in the beginning with God" (St. John 1:1-2). Modern scholarship has tried to explain the miracle of Jesus through a unique plan which would divide the miracle into two parts and then explain it. Instead of wrestling with the age-old problem of the human and divine natures in Jesus Christ, some scholars have made Him both the historic Jesus and the Heavenly Christ. Jesus, the Man of History, was on the earth and endured the afflictions of the world in which He lived. He grew weary and hungry, and even wept at moments of great grief. On the other hand, He was considered as the Heavenly Christ. He was God's exalted one, the Lord and Savior about whom Paul spoke so freely and fully. The Heavenly Christ was the Eternal One, God's gift to the world and heaven's agent of grace and salvation. Yet when the scholars and theologians have arranged their respective categories and have defined the personality of Jesus Christ in terms of their own outlooks, and when the humble preacher has finished his story about the strange man dying on a cross, we still have before us the great redemptive personality on which the faith of every believer rests. We must leave any doubts for others. In spite of the disagreements in the attempts to explain Jesus, the church is at one in accepting the fact of the life and message of Jesus because He is the solid rock on which every congregation of Christians stands and is the power through and by whom the work of salvation is done.

In her admiration for the message of Jesus the church does not turn back the pages of history or lose her future in a worship of the past or a preoccupation with the present. By the highest standard of thought and a most lofty ethical concept born of the purest conscience of men, Jesus is still a future reality, a standard of life not yet attained. In spite of the changes in human history He remains a great moral and spiritual force. He is truth, and truth is timeless. As the revelation of God, eternity alone can contain the riches of His spirit. A writer once surveyed the achievements of the past and catalogued the work of many of the creative spirits in history, concluding that our modern age has incorporated the best of the past and many changes have resulted because of this. After raising a question, he gives his answer:

What has been the effect of these immense changes upon our attitudes to Jesus: We reply that in spite of these extraordinary revolutions in our intellectual world Jesus still captivates the human race with the splendor of the divine that radiates from Him. His image has become brighter and more vivid—that is all. Still He waits with a welcome all His own for those who seek God, waits for those who seek the true humanity.[2]

As we behold the message and the man, we are convinced that the miracle of Jesus Christ reaches the highest peak of spiritual significance in the work of the Cross. The Cross is the symbol of the Christian religion for Protestants and Roman Catholics. The Cross embraces the total life of Christ. It is the symbol representing the epitome of that whole divine transaction which theologians have called the atonement. Here the work of redemption is brought to a focal point, and the whole plan of salvation is revealed with clarity and power. Men may approach

---

[2] *Ibid*, p. 166.

the Cross of Christ with varying attitudes, philosophies and even different levels of understanding, but when they look at it they see a great redemptive action. Theologians have differed profoundly in their analyses of the message of the Cross, but the Christian church has found elements of agreement, compelling forces about which all believers may sing together and embrace with appreciation and joy.

In the presence of the Cross there is no place for personal pride or boasting. Here humanism has no message and has never felt at home. For the very presence of the Cross is a stern rebuke to human pride and a firm denial of human self-sufficiency. If the ability for the redemption of self had been in the human race, there would not have been any necessity for the extreme price paid by our Lord and Master. If the resources of salvation had been in man, then the tragedy of the Cross would not have called man out of himself to look to God for salvation and deliverance. If the moral and spiritual state of the fallen race of Adam had not been so depraved, the divine outreach as expressed in the Cross would not have been necessary. If there had been any easier way out, God through His wisdom and power would have employed it. But the wretchedness of man could only be answered by the worthiness of God as expressed in His love and mercy on the Cross.

When he looks at the holiness and divine self-giving of the Cross, a sinful man must confess: "I am not worthy." His plight is similar to that of the weary, poverty-stricken, dirty, dejected, and lonely prodigal son. When he saw once again the tender face of a loving father and saw the robe, the ring, and all of the blessings of the father's house from which he had once departed, he said: "I am not worthy to be called thy son. Make me one of thy hired servants." The experiences of the far country had broken his pride. He had followed his pride; it had led him away from a place of love to a strange, cruel and degrading land. A riotous life among loveless friends had consumed his goods, and the resulting life of need had taught him how poor and helpless

he was away from his father's house. The long hours in the filth
and misery of the swine's pen had told the young man how
stupid and how wretched he was. He had tried his possessions;
now they had been wasted and all was lost. He was left in
poverty. What then remained for him to trust? Only the rugged
road of humility, leading from that pit of the past back to his
father's house, remained. Only in humility could a once proud
son stand before his father and say: "I am not worthy. I come
not in the name of merit, but in the name of mercy. I come not
by the power of what I am, but by the strength of what you
are." The poverty of the son was more than matched by the
inner riches of his loving father.

The Cross of Jesus Christ reveals both the helpless plight of
lost mankind and the redemptive care of its loving father. Here
the father goes a step further than did the father in the story of
the prodigal son. The father in the story remained at home but
graciously and sympathetically received the son on his return.
In the case of our redemption, the Father in Jesus Christ left
home, went to the far country, and finally went to the filthy pen
where the lost son sat in shame and disgrace. He rescued the
boy, brought him home, cleansed him, dressed him, fed him,
and — above all — owned him. The whole story of Jesus seems
to say to the lost humanity: "This is my son who was lost but
is found, was dirty but is now clean, was guilty and condemned,
now justified; was dead, but is now alive." Among all the things
that happened to the prodigal son in Luke's story the greatest
was the father's ownership. It was his son-ship that the prodigal
boy thought he had utterly lost. The greatest thing that happens to sinful men in the presence of the Cross is the Father's
ownership. He says, "These are my children. They have been
forgiven and they are now restored."

In the next place, we approach the Cross of Christ in a spirit
of surrender, each believer saying to Him: "Make me one of
Thy hired servants. Allow me to work for you. Give me employment in Thy Kingdom, for experience has taught that it is

far better to be a hired servant in my Father's house than to be a free lancer in a far country." This is self-denial at its best. Here is no contention for the privilege of son-ship but a request for an opportunity to serve as a servant. The only approach that man can make to God in the sight of the Cross is one of complete self-denial and self-surrender. To the Cross we can bring nothing of value. Whatever we might possess is of little value in the shadow of the Cross.

In Thomas More's *Utopia* gold has little or no value for this new community. It has lost its lustre. There are other values by which men are considered worthy. In the shadow of the Cross there are also new values that are considered far above material things. They are spiritual, not material. Here material things gain a new significance, for they are used in the interest of human uplift, and dedicated to the service of God. The poet expressed it well when he said: "Nothing in my hands I bring, simply to the Cross I cling." While it is beautiful poetry, the statement is more. Its meaning goes deeper than the imagery born of words. It goes to the very heart of life. This statement is great theology. When men can learn this lesson, a golden age will dawn among the believers in Christ.

There is discord among men who claim a place under the Cross because they approach the Cross with full hands: full of old possessions, old traditions, old materialistic philosophies, preconceived notions, prejudices, and many other things which are foreign to the gospel of the Cross. Some have approached the Cross without receiving the blessings of divine grace because they have tried to bring these holdings of the past with them. But man's natural possessions will perish with his flesh. He who trusts in gold and silver and puts his confidence in material things will subject justice, freedom, and human personalities to these perishing materials. In the presence of the Cross material things have a minor place.

Others have approached the Cross but missed the benediction of it because they came holding on to their old traditions of nationality, race, and custom. A strictly national or racial church is not the church of the Cross of Jesus Christ. It may be an exclusive social club where people of the same race and nationality meet to renew their pledges to keep themselves pure and separated from others, but we do not come to the Cross to defend blood, race, or nation. Rather, we approach it looking for the defense that is ours alone through the life and blood of Jesus Christ and saying: "Nothing in my hands I bring, simply to the Cross I cling." We cannot bring faith in our own goodness, our own personal character, or the goodness of family. We cannot come with pride in religious tradition. At the foot of the Cross one brings nothing but faith in God and confidence in the saving power of Jesus Christ. We may approach the Cross with high expectations. We expect the miracle of redemption. We look forward to the restoration of the lost divine image and seek with unquestioned hope the fellowship of the Kingdom of God. This expectation rests on our faith, on what God had promised, and on what He has already done through our Lord Jesus Christ. Paul brings this expectation to focus in a statement of faith that becomes more than a promise. It is a reality of grace, a fact of divine redemption, and an eternal reward for all who accept the claims of the gospel and who embrace the Cross of Jesus Christ. He sees a permanent fellowship between the believer and his God because there are no powers strong enough to separate a trusting soul from the love of Christ. Paul asks his searching question and finds the answer in the eternal things of God.

Who shall separate us from the love of Christ? shall tribulation, or distress, or persecution, or famine, or nakedness, or peril, or sword? As it is written, For Thy sake we are killed all the day long; we are accounted as sheep for the slaughter. Nay, in all these things we are more than conquerors through Him that loved us. For I am persuaded that neither death, nor life, nor angels, nor principalities, nor powers, nor things present, nor things to come, nor height, nor depth, nor any other creature, shall be able to separate us from the love of God, which is in Christ Jesus our Lord (Romans 8:35-39).

What we seek is under the shadow of the Cross where forces are available that will hold believers in union with Christ and in union one with the other. Believers in Christ share a common redemption through the power of the Cross of Jesus Christ. Differences there will be, errors and mistakes are sure to come, insights will be as varied as are intellectual capacities and moral gifts, but the central fact of divine concern for human salvation is one of the mountain peaks in human history where all believers can gather in peace and in joy.

7

THE HOLY SPIRIT

THROUGHOUT OUR BIBLE we recognize an agency of the Divine Mind at work among the children of men. This agency or influence is called by different names but the purposes and functions are very much the same. The Spirit of God, the Word of God, or His messengers are sent forth to assist in the work of creation and the preservation, guidance, and protection of His people. Through the work of God's Spirit His will is done, His protection is given, His comfort is made available, His love and His concern communicated to the world of things and to His human creatures.

In the Book of Genesis there is an agency of God employed to help in the creative act: "And the Spirit of God moved upon the face of the waters" (Genesis 1:2). The Spirit of God here goes forth as an agency of creativity producing the world that is. In many cases God works through angels. They are His ministers and His messengers. The angels were often sent forth to bless and to protect the servants of God. "Bless ye the Lord, ye His angels that excell in strength, that do His commandments, harkening unto the voice of His word" (Psalms 103:20). In the story of Daniel angels were the agencies sent forth to protect a persecuted servant of God. Daniel was not destroyed in the den of lions because God by His angels had shut the lions' mouths.

My God has sent His angel, and has shut the lions's mouths, that they have not hurt me: for as much as before Him innocency was found in me; and also before thee, oh king, have I done no hurt (Daniel 6:22).

Throughout the Old Testament as well as in some parts of the New, angels are the agents of God working for and among men. According to the writer of the Book of Hebrews, angels were spirits sent forth to serve those who were heirs of salvation. Says he of them: "Are they not all ministering spirits, sent forth to minister for them who shall be heirs of salvation" (Hebrews 1:14). In the New Testament and in the history of the Christian church the Holy Spirit becomes the power by and through which God works in the hearts and minds of believers.

The work of redemption so nobly begun by the Jesus of history was not completed in the three and a half years of His public ministry. The treatises written by Luke and the other synoptic writers as well as the author of the Fourth Gospel dealt with the things that Jesus did and taught during His earthly ministry. When He said "It is finished," Jesus did not mean that the work of the Kingdom of God was consummated and that the whole field of the gospel potential had been thoroughly covered. He meant that His part in the program as an earthly messenger had come to an end. But he knew there remained much more to be done before God's promised Kingdom would be fulfilled. Jesus had finished a phase of the work. The additional work for world redemption and for the development of the Christian community was to be done through the Holy Spirit. God, in the building of His promised Kingdom, has revealed himself through three modes of being: that of Father, Son, and the Holy Ghost. We have already observed the work of God the Father and God the Son, and now our task is to observe the work of God the Holy Spirit.

The functional relationship between God and the Holy Spirit has occasioned wide variations of theological opinion, but there is profound agreement on the place of the Holy Spirit in the

Christian church. It is this latter aspect of the subject that shall be our great concern.

What is the work of the Holy Spirit? It is impossible to draw a fast line between the work of the Holy Spirit as an agent of God in His acts of creation and the work of the Holy Spirit in the public ministry of Jesus Christ, for in both of these aspects of the work the Holy Spirit was very much in evidence. He was present in the work of creation and at the very conception of the child Jesus. After the baptism of Jesus it was the Holy Spirit that proclaimed His son-ship, and the work that Jesus did during His public career on earth was the result of the anointment of the Spirit of God. But during the period of His earthly ministry the personality and message of Jesus held the center of attention. It was after the resurrection of Jesus that the work of the Kingdom was carried on by the Holy Spirit. In brief, the work of the Holy Spirit was the continuation of the work of the Kingdom of God as began by Jesus Christ. This includes the development of the church and the church's mission to the world and finally the winning of the world to the will of God. There are several approaches that are employed by the Holy Spirit in His task, many of which were promised to the disciples by Jesus. The first phase of this work was to quicken the memory of the believers to the things of the Kingdom that Jesus taught. According to the Fourth Gospel He makes this promise:

But the comforter, which is the holy ghost, whom the Father will send in my name, He shall teach you all things, and bring all things to your remembrance, whatsoever I have said unto you (St. John 14:26).

One of the great dangers that confronted the disciples after the departure of Jesus was forgetting what Jesus had taught them and thereby exposing themselves to the errors of mis-statements of the message of Jesus. Having been left in an environment that was hostile to Jesus, living face to face with people who had sought not only to misinterpret Him while He lived but who had labored to destroy Him, the disciples were in danger of losing the original image of Jesus and substituting a psuedo-image that was contrary to truth. Jesus left no written record, and all of His teachings had to be kept in the minds and souls of those who heard Him. If memory had failed them, the gospel of Jesus Christ would have been lost to future generations. Therefore, it was the work of the Holy Spirit not only to teach but to guard well the memory of the disciples against the intrusion of evil notions that might come and steal the central place in the minds of the believers and thus cause the precious seed of the gospel of truth to be substituted by empty fables. As the angel guarded the ancient Garden of Eden to keep men from entering the once holy spot, so the Holy Spirit guards the sacred precincts of the minds against the mastery of error and evil.

Not only did the Holy Spirit guard the mind but it entered the sacred chambers of the same, cleansing, purifying, nurturing, and keeping alive the spiritual gems implanted by Jesus Christ Himself. It was the Holy Spirit that kept the mind fertile with visions, dreams, and expectations of a fuller revelation of God. The Holy Spirit did not allow the minds of the early apostles to be overpowered by sinful drives and to be poisoned by the evil one. The Holy Spirit was present both in the sub-conscious and conscious mind for purification and edification, for if the Holy Spirit had ever departed from these believers they would have lost the vision of Jesus Christ and their empty minds would have been peopled with the demons of error and sin, and this second state would have been worse than the first. The Spirit then not only protected and cleansed the minds of these early believers, but it also quickened them in the message of Jesus.

Historians have told how the gospel of Jesus lived for a period as oral tradition. The spoken words of Jesus were kept alive only in the memory of the apostles and believers who heard Him, and were passed on from one to another by means of fiery testimony. This was not due to rote memory but rather to the fact that the Spirit of God had kept the story straight and alive in the minds and hearts of these humble preachers, and their task was to pass it on. The only documents that Jesus left were the plastic minds of His disciples on which He had stamped the image of His being and wrote the good news of deliverance for a lost world. And the only parchment on which the first apostles could write were the receptive souls of the people who listened to their story.

The Holy Spirit dictated the message of the early preachers of the Cross as well as prepared the soil in which the gospel seeds were cast. Long before the church was in possession of a written word of God she was sustained by an oral testimony that depended on a memory enriched by the Holy Spirit. The resurrection event and the attending dynamic faith resulted from the work that the Holy Spirit had done in His contact with the material and the physical. As the Spirit of God descended upon ancient chaos and formed the cosmic order, so the Holy Spirit descended upon the human potential of the early believers and brought into being that dynamic fellowship called the church. The church as a heavenly promise existed before the world was born, but as a living dynamic faith the church was the result of the work of the Holy Spirit on the minds of men.

The written word or the Holy Bible came as a result of the work of the Holy Spirit on the souls of men enabling them to set down on parchment what had so long been passed on from mind to mind as the living truth proclaimed by Jesus Christ. The Holy Spirit had no message of its own without the basic truth proclaimed by Jesus Christ. On this truth the Holy Spirit built.

The Holy Spirit also had the role of Comforter of the early believers. The departure of Jesus as a living objective reality did much to trouble the souls of His disciples. They faced disappointment and discouragement because Jesus did not overthrow the ruling powers of the times and set up an earthly kingdom. Some had even inquired of Him if He were going to restore to Israel her golden age. "When they were come together they asked Him, saying, Lord, wilt thou at this time restore again the kingdom of Israel?" (Acts 1:6). They were further disappointed that Jesus did not physically remain with them as a worker of miracles, as an advisor and protector. His departure left an aching void that no speculation could adequately fill. As had been promised, the Holy Ghost came to comfort the believers and to show them that God was still with them and at work in the world advancing the cause of His Kingdom. The early church soon learned that the work of the Kingdom and the divine concern were not limited to a physical presence but that God could work through His Holy Spirit as He had done through His living Son. The believers now learned that the fate of God's Kingdom did not depend upon what men did or could do to a human being or to a God-man. God as spirit could work through a physical presence, but He could work as well through His Holy Spirit. This was necessary to aid the early church in understanding that God was not dependent on material things to accomplish the spiritual things of His kingdom. Any belief that would limit God to work through a physical presence would be, however refined, the basis for a kind of materialism. In the Holy Spirit, the church had a trustworthy guide. The disciples were not left to flounder and to drift for the Holy Spirit was always present to guide them through the storms of life and into the formation of the church. He taught them both the importance and the method of spiritual togetherness.

One of the greatest, if not the greatest, social miracles in history is the creation of the Christian church, a fellowship whose only purpose is the spiritual enrichment of its members and the creative response of every member of that fellowship to things spiritual and their right relationship with God the source of all life. The church makes everything else secondary to the task of creative fulfillment of each member and to the redemption and purification of all men. The church transcends the barriers of race and nationality and proclaims the unity of mankind and the oneness of all through the life and blood of Jesus Christ our Lord. There is no other fellowship in the world based on the unselfish love of all for each and each for all as is the church.

The Book of Acts is more than the acts of the apostles. It is in reality the acts of the Holy Spirit. Beginning with the dynamic power of Pentecost one sees what a difference the presence of the Holy Spirit makes in the lives of individual members and in the fellowship as a whole. Men who had been weak are now strong. Some who had been afraid to testify to their knowledge and relationship with Jesus in the presence of others are now courageous enough to proclaim the truth of Christ before officials of state and leaders of organized religion. Those who were once afraid to suffer with Jesus are now glad to suffer and even die that the gospel story might be told.

The early church demonstrated that the mission of the kingdom was not by might, but by the eternal spirit of God. The holy plan of redemption so well worked out by the sacrificial life, death, and resurrection of Jesus Christ was now to be applied by the Holy Spirit. A study of the Book of Acts does reveal somewhat the nature of the pagan world in which the early church had to live, but the comfort, guidance, and certainty given by the Holy Spirit proved more than a match for the hostile world about. Those who were aflamed by the spirit went everywhere proclaiming the good news of the Kingdom of God and lifting the dead in sin to a new life of faith and hope. Given such an influence the messengers of the gospel *need not* shrink from any task and *will not* retreat before any hostile powers but will go forth to face every peril knowing full well that the gates of hell cannot prevail against them and that principalities and powers will not stop the victorious march of truth.

Across the centuries it has been and still is the work of the Holy Spirit that has kept the church marching forward as an army with banners. She marches because she has a mastery that materialism cannot control and misery can never silence. The growth of the church has been a growth from within. When men have obeyed the inner compulsion of the Spirit of God they have gone forth proclaiming the truth of divine salvation. This has been done and is still being done because of God's deep concern for man, the object of salvation.

8

THE CHRISTIAN CONCEPTION OF MAN

IT IS OBVIOUS that man is the primary object of salvation. If there were no other testimony aside from that significant statement in St. John 3:16,[1] we would have sufficient proof that man is the subject of God's concern in the redemptive act. The world that God loved so much that He sent His Son for its salvation was a world that had the mental power to believe or not to believe, the moral capacity to accept or to reject the plan of salvation. "Whosoever believeth in Him" did not refer to inanimate matter or to animals incapable of mental choices. A believing world is a human world. Furthermore this world is a world that is dependent on life and an heir to eternity. It is not our purpose here to deal with the great anthropological questions of history but to give a few brief statements about the nature of man that represents the Christian point of view.

There are several things regarding the nature of man that all Christians hold in common. If he were less than what the Christian message ascribes to his nature, man would be beyond the reach of the work of grace as revealed in the Gospel of Jesus Christ. If he were more than the Christian religion claims for him, man would be beyond the need that Jesus saw present in him. Man's self-sufficiency would have rendered him too rich in mental, moral and spiritual equipment to have any need for the redemptive gifts from God through Jesus Christ.

---

[1] "For God so loved the world, that he gave his only begotten Son, that whosoever believeth in him should not perish, but have everlasting life."

What is this Christian conception of man? What is man that he should be the concern of God and the object of the redemptive work of Jesus Christ? What are the liabilities of his nature that make him a creature in need of divine help? What drives him to seek the resources and the refuge that are in Christ Jesus? What are those values resident in man that make him the pearl of great price and the deserving lamb that the great Shepherd loves and seeks? What is that mind and that quality of life in him that enables him to respond to the redemptive outreach of God through Jesus Christ? What of those ears by which he is blessed to hear the word of God and what of the eyes through which he may see the things of God?

Showing one the spiritual values of the Kingdom of God would be a waste of time if one could not see. Telling the story of redemption is a fruitless effort if one has not the ears to hear. Man, the object of the Christian message, is afflicted but has a soundness that enables him to respond to the medicine of mercy and to the sustenance of grace. He is poor yet potentially rich; blind yet seeing, and there is in him both the mud of humanity and the marble of divinity. Man as an entity is both a creature of negatives and of positives, possessing liabilities and assets at the same time. The Christian religion deals with man as a whole and does not demand of him the death of his desires nor the annihilation of his central self. Unlike one school of Buddhism it does not conclude that all existence is suffering. Nor does it seek to insulate the self from the actualities of human existence through a theory and practice of world denial. The Christian religion affirms man in both his weaknesses and his strengths by offering a remedy for his weakness and appealing to the nobility of his strength.

Yet the first aspect of man's nature is the negative. He is a creature of needs. The Christian message begins on the assumption that man is incomplete by nature, needing the patience of growth in order to come to the level of human fulfillment. He is dependent, unworthy, poor, lost, and blind. This deficiency is not lodged in the emotions and in the physical nature of man alone. It is found at the very core of his being. Reinhold Niebuhr says:

The Christian estimate of human evil is so serious precisely because it places evil at the very centre of human personality: in the will. This evil cannot be regarded complacently as the inevitable consequence of his finiteness or the fruits of his involvement in the contingencies and necessities of nature. Sin is occasioned precisely by the fact that man refuses to admit his "creatureliness" and to acknowledge himself as merely a member of a total unity of life. He pretends to be more than he is.[2]

It seems that man has misused some of the basic things of his nature; he has employed his highest talents in acts of rebellion against the God who made him. Says Mr. Niebuhr further:

The essence of man is his freedom. Sin is committed in that freedom. . . . The freedom of his spirit causes him to break the harmonies of nature and the pride of his spirit prevents him from establishing a new harmony. The freedom of his spirit enables him to use the forces and processes of nature creatively; but his failure to observe the limits of his finite existence causes him to divide the forms and restraints of both nature and reason.[3]

These statements by a modern scholar are much in harmony with the Genesis story regarding the tragic fall of man. As a sinner, man made the wrong choice and destroyed some of his basic values. By these acts of his volition he lost a garden and by losing a vital fellowship he won for himself misery, solitude, pain, and death. Paul seems to trace the penalty of sin back to the fallen father of mankind in the following words: ". . . in Adam all die" (1 Corinthians 15:22). This is the source of the incompleteness of man. He is a depraved and fallen creature.

[2] Reinhold Niebuhr, *The Nature and Destiny of Man*, I (New York, Charles Scribners Sons, 1941), p. 16.
[3] *Ibid*, p. 17.

The writer of the Book of Genesis describes man at his beginning as having the wealth of being and a fruitful garden of un- limited possibilities. Later, the same writer explains the incom- pleteness of man's nature and the sinfulness of his character in terms of a great fall. He is a sinner who has misused his precious assets and has won guilt for himself, coming far short of the glory of God. Paul testified that: "all have sinned and come short of the glory of God" (Romans 3:23). The divine image is marred. Our Eden of moral and spiritual potential has been partially lost, and our human worthiness has now become un- worthy. Sin, then, is an act of choosing the wrong in the presence of the right. It is an act of choosing the better when the best is available.

But more than an act, sin is a state. It is a state of spiritual degeneration, a state of inner rebellion against the highest in nature, in life, and in God. The human will is as corrupt as the human emotions. The power of choice has been so weakened that in the hour that man would choose the good, evil is always there to plague and misdirect his efforts and his intentions. When he would rise to obey the urgent directions of the "oughtness" of conscience, his feet are found in stocks. He cannot go where he ought to go and cannot do what he ought to do. It matters not where we begin the story of man; sooner or later we come to the point of human poverty, human depravity, human weak- ness, sickness, and death. If we do not agree with others who think of religion as a feeling of dependence, we must admit that from the negative side it arises out of a sense of need and grows in a consciousness of unworthiness. If man has started the upward march from the lower order of being to the heights of a more complete life, then we must admit that some obstacles have hindered him and some weights from the distant past have overburdened him, seriously retarding his upward march.

But this story of the needs of man is not a complete story of man without reference to his potential strength, to his moral and spiritual possibilities. He is more than flesh and blood. He is much more than an examination of the material order reveals. Man is both a spirit, possessing a soul, as well as a physical being; he has been made in the image of God. He is a citizen in the kingdom of spiritual values. He is a creature of faith, not the helpless victim of the past or the cringing slave of the present, but one who looks toward a future made bright by the grace of God. Man yields not to the limitations of today for he has the unlimited possibilities of his tomorrow by the help of God. It is true he lives by bread, but it is equally true that he does not live by bread alone. The message of Jesus is addressed to the nature of man. When He speaks of the wealth of a man's soul, Jesus appeals to the best that there is in humanity. Yet the gospel of Christ recognizes the worst that also haunts man's being. Consequently, there is no other gospel for sinful men but this gospel that recognizes both the human plight and the human possibility. When he would correct the gospel heresy in the churches of Galatia, Paul told them there was no other gospel for human salvation.

> But though we, or an angel from heaven, preach any other gospel unto you than that which we have preached unto you, let him be accursed (Galatians 1:8).

The wisdom of man could not produce it, and the genius of the learned could find no substitute for it. Said Paul:

> Beware lest any man spoil you through philosophy and vain deceit, after the tradition of men, after the rudiments of the world, and not after Christ (Colossians 2:8).

For Paul knew such was possible, and it still is. When believers have been set at war each against the other, it has happened because they have been spoiled by some kind of worldly philosophy and captured by deceit, the fruit of which is both vicious and vain.

The message of the gospel of Christ is addressed to man as he is, and not as he can become. The church is agreed that this gospel of Christ is the good news for lost men and the ready remedy for the sinful nature of all human beings. This gospel has been shaped by God Himself to meet the needs of man in all ages until the book of human existence is closed, and the end has come to the struggles of man. Man is on his way to the heights of God, to a destiny beyond the dust. Flesh and blood belong to the earth, and the elements shall return to element, but the soul of man is endowed with the everlasting life that redemption has made secure.

III

THE CONSTRUCTIVE USE OF ACCEPTED AREAS OF AGREEMENTS

BUILDING FELLOWSHIP ON AGREEMENTS

By THE LIGHT of the facts of history and the truths of life we cannot deny that there are areas of profound, inescapable, and universal agreement among Christian believers. We have noted that the Christian church is already in possession of more than areas of conflict and confusion. Certain questions arise concerning these areas of agreement. Shall we subordinate them to the disagreements that have plagued the church throughout its history and continue to seek ways by which we may still disagree on the fundamentals of the Christian faith? Or shall we accept the areas of agreement and build on them?

All too often we have tried to be different when the facts did not warrant it, and have overemphasized areas of disagreement in order to remain distinct from others who have approached the Christian message in a different light or tradition. Some have feared that confessing agreements with other religious groups might occasion the loss of prestige, or even the loss of some of their members to other religious groups. But here we must remind ourselves that the object of our struggle is not the victory of one religious group over another. Our purpose must be more inclusive, more noble. It must be concerned with the total realization of the Kingdom of God. The life of a religious denomination need not depend on competition with other groups nor upon a constant declaration of one's orthodox position accompanied by its alleged authority. A group must no longer seek to arrive at a position of power by the process of negating other groups. It is a most wholesome attitude of mind for Christian believers to know and seek to magnify those things which they hold in common with other believers. A contrary approach is the way of defeatism which tends to retard the progressive work of the Kingdom of love and righteousness.

Living with agreements tends to develop a wider feeling of kinship and aids in the establishment of vital relationships. Believers are brothers at the level of agreements, and the simple recognition of this fact will draw believers closer together than all the debating, theological hairsplitting, and resolutions could ever do. From the standpoint of these positive agreements believers may see and interpret their differences. They will find that their differences are not as striking as they once thought and not as difficult as they once believed. They will surely find that the things on which they do agree are nearer to the heart of reality than those things on which they do not agree. The need for compromise and for the modification of dogmas will be greatly reduced because the bases already exist for a true relationship that will render unity a possibility and fellowship a spiritual reality.

As we take the accepted agreements, build on them, embrace them, and employ them in a community of interest in quest of deeper areas of kinship, the results will be the discovery and tapping of new moral and spiritual energy by which the work of the Kingdom of God will be greatly advanced. The work of Christians does not become a task of political strategy and of administrative readjustments, but rather an act of spiritual renewal with a progressive revival of religion both in individual life and in the Christian community. Is it too much to say that whenever men work for the cause of the Kingdom of God they are brothers in spite of the rituals of their churches, the languages which they speak or the religious traditions in which they were born and nurtured? For in the light of the prophetic words and deeds of Jesus, the Kingdom of God cannot come to pass through evil agencies, and the immortal life cannot be brought to full fruition by the use of methods on which Satan depends to build his empire.

No church denomination is an island unto itself. Beneath the changing tide of circumstances, the flux of human emotions, and the manifold experiences of everyday life, there is a basic reality that unites the hearts of all believers. This is not a unity to be worked out through the genius of political leaders or theologians. This is a unity that is broader than time and as eternal as the spirit of truth. A modern author has made a statement that might well be applied to the Christian church in this context:

"No man is an island," wrote the poet-churchman, John Donne. Might he not better have said, every man is an island, but islands are not what they appear to be: isolated bodies of land. For if one presses beneath the surface of the water one will come upon a land base that unites these individual bodies of land with all land.[1]

The time has come when Christians must go beneath the surface of the waters of differences in order to find that land of spiritual life that is joined to the land of divine truth where they can build. According to St. Luke, Jesus did not limit the messengers of His kingdom to those who were working in His immediate company of disciples. Whoever participated in the work of the Kingdom was joined to Him and to His disciples.

And John answered and said, Master, we saw one casting out devils in Thy name; and we forbade him, because he followeth not with us. And Jesus said unto him, forbid him not: for he that is not against us is for us (Luke 9:49-50).

According to this testimony, there was no question about the efficiency of the work that the man in the story was doing. He was not deceiving the people. He was not imitating those who had real authority and power over the demons. He *was* casting out devils. He did not do this by the power of Satan; he did it in the name of Jesus Christ.

[1] Bernard E. Meland, *The Realities of Faith: The Revolution in Culture Forms* (New York, Oxford University Press, 1962), p. 231.

John and the other disciples had their spiritual authority in
the name of Jesus Christ. The report was: "We saw one casting
out devils IN THY NAME." This alone should have been
enough to instruct John and the other disciples about their
oneness and kinship, for all of them were agreed that the source
of their authority was in the same Lord and Master. But John
and the disciples allowed the slight difference to control their
thinking and their action; the only reason given was "because he
followed not with us." They decided he did not have the same
authority because he was not in their company. This story is
true of life today.

The only argument that many modern Christians have against
other religious groups is the fact that they "follow not with us."
They are not in our company; they do not recite our creed;
they do not walk in our religious tradition. But unlike His
disciples, Jesus did not concentrate on the area of differences,
but on the single point of agreement: he was working as they
were, through the same divine source. The conclusion to which
Jesus came was a conclusion born of the fact of the established
agreement of the man at work with Himself and His disciples.
Jesus warned the disciples not to oppose the man, "for he that
is not against us is for us." He that agrees with our source of
power is with us.

According to the Fourth Gospel, Jesus recognized other sheep
that were not of this particular fold. Said He:

And other sheep I have, which are not of this fold: them also I must
bring, and they shall hear my voice; and there shall be one fold, and
one shepherd (John 10:16).

All are sheep; they are owned and controlled by the same
shepherd. They differ only in the location in which they are
found. There may be many folds but one shepherd. The fact of
the folds does not determine the kinship of the sheep. We must
not determine sheep by the style of the pen or by the location of

the fold. We cannot increase the shepherd's ownership by seeking to herd all the sheep into one physical pen, nor can we bring all the sheep together by theological gymnastics and religious short cuts. This remains the work of the Great Shepherd. He said: "Them I must also bring and they shall hear my voice." Without the power of the Christ and the sound of His compelling voice, there is no human agency that can make one fold out of the sheep of all the pastures of the world. We must remember that we are one in the fact that we have the same Shepherd; and we must agree that His power as well as His unlimited and gracious presence may be felt among us.

A brief review of the cardinal principles of the Christian church will reveal that the things on which we agree are given to us by God through His Spirit and through the mission of Jesus Christ. It is the work that man has done in the church in his attempt to interpret and define the meaning of Christian life that has been the occasion of the many divisions within the church. As members of different denominations, we have learned to concentrate on our differences and have become determined to hold on to the doctrines that distinguish our group from another. We must now learn how to react positively to the undisputed agreements among us. We must also learn that such positive reactions do not in any way reflect indifference toward our own denomination, nor should they be construed as disloyalty to the tradition in which we have been nurtured. Rather, they should be interpreted as our growth in Christian understanding.

In order to take this step, we must develop a new mind: a mind that is not only concerned with our particular denomination but with the great universals of the Christian religion on which there is unquestioned agreement. This quest for agreement must always be objective. It must never be for the purpose of claiming kinship with another in order to seek to fall heir to any position, prestige, or power within the group under discussion. It is not a study of a family tree in order to establish kinship to a family fortune. The study is for the purpose of establishing kinship with our brethren in the common task of cross-bearing for Christ and in the work of world redemption. This requires a new courage not only to face the criticisms of the members within one's own group who are not yet ready to put the general truths of the Kingdom before narrow sectarian concerns but also to follow in the Kingdom-way that the Spirit of God may lead us in the future, whatever the hazards and costs. Loyalty to one's church, theology, and denominational program is no sin and should be encouraged. But any denominational or other type of loyalty that in any way leads to a conflict with loyalty to Christ is unwise and should be discouraged.

Differences between religious groups have been the subject of much discussion in the past and in the present. In the future, more stress should be put on accepted agreements among Christians everywhere. This should lead to a closer kinship among believers. Dialogue between different religious groups should go beyond the study of their particular doctrines; it should go into the area of basic Christian agreements. This kind of dialogue will do more than lift the God-given agreements into the center of thought and action. It will also shed some helpful light on some of the historic differences. There is a dialogue already going on between Protestant and Roman Catholic thinkers in an attempt to understand their respective teachings. This study has yielded much fruit for good. Perhaps this is the beginning which will lead to a more thorough study of the areas of agreement between them, and perhaps their theologians will be permitted to write a joint story on the things upon which they do agree. This would make an interesting and rich body of literature. Research into the history and theology of the Protestant and Roman Catholic Churches, with the view of finding common terms and common grounds, will make a significant contribution to the ecumenical movement and will be a step toward a strong world Christian fellowship. Yet this type of study requires not only courage but an objectivity which rises above the psychological limitations of strictly denominational thinking.

The Christian church may rejoice in the fact that in spite of differences she is in possession of the material for the making of a world fellowship. We have observed the basic agreements that can be used as the common object around which we may rally a common interest and concern, and thereby build a world-wide Christian fellowship. In any fellowship two things are most essential: a common mind and a kindred feeling. Both of these are achieved in the process of reacting creatively to the same object. An illustration of this may be drawn from the birth and growth of the United States of America, which began as a settlement of many different people from different countries of Europe. The settlers in this new land were soon drawn together by a common desire for freedom which welded them into one great national community. Their former loyalties were soon transferred from the old to this new country. To make this new land and this new community into an ideal republic was the object of their striving.

The country and the cause fired these new settlers to labor and suffer for the realization of their dreams, and in the process they achieved a common mind. Now they thought the same thoughts just as they embraced the same ideals and espoused the same democratic cause. If they were to succeed they knew they had to think together, plan together, and work together and soon what were once individual thoughts and plans for the separate colonies were merged into the thought of the nation as a whole. Without this psychological process a new nation could not have been constructed out of thirteen scattered and separate colonies; the thirteen willed to become one and thus the many were merged into one whole.

In the same manner, Christians—believers from different denominations, traditions, and cultures—may accept the unquestioned fact of the existence of those divine resources that are given unto them. They too may learn to go forth and labor for the same task and in the process acquire a new mind, a kindred mind in all things spiritual. Paul knew that all that he said to the church at Philippi regarding embracing the things of Christ would not mean much and could not be retained by them for long unless they finally learned to think the thoughts of Christ Himself. They had to have within them the mind of Christ. Hence Paul said to them:

Let this mind be in you, which was also in Christ Jesus (Philippians 2:5).

When we embrace the same Christ and venture to proclaim the same gospel in the interest of the same Kingdom of God we will develop the same mind. It is clear that there can be no world-wide Christian fellowship without a world-wide Christian mind, and there can be no world-wide Christian mind unless there is a world-wide Christian thought, and there can be no world-wide Christian thought unless there are world-wide Christian verities and virtues on which believers can agree. In the light of the above one may read with a new appreciation Paul's summons to Christian thought in the following words:

Finally, brethren, whatsoever things are true, whatsoever things are honest, whatsoever things are just, whatsoever things are pure, whatsoever things are lovely, whatsoever things are of good report; if there be any virtue, if there be any praise, think on these things (Philippians 4:8).

In Christ Jesus we now know what things are true, what things are honest, what things are just, what things are pure, what things are lovely, and what things are the bases of a good report. Now we know as believers on what to think and therefore may enjoy the mind of Christ as a guide and a directive as we experience together one dynamic world Christian fellowship. But a fellowship is not based wholly on the rational approach to the problems at hand. It is also a kinship of emotions. People in the same fellowship feel a kinship that is deeper than the forces that would tend to estrange. Common experiences tend to inspire like feeling tones of life. People who are united in bonds of love soon experience sensations of security, responsibility, suffering, and joy.

They may have a feeling of anxiety when they are confronted with a threat to their continued existence.When they look on forces that are hostile to the cause they have embraced, they experience a feeling of urgency that may result in grief or in a determination to make the greatest sacrifice for the victory of their cause. There is a common sorrow for failures and a common joy for every victory.

In the early church the believers had all things in common. This refers to more than their sharing of their economic goods. The total emotional experiences of life were held in common so that if one member of the fellowship was troubled, they would meet in privacy and pray to God for his deliverance. They sought release for those who were bound in prison cells and would extend a helping hand to those in need. Also, when they saw signs of spiritual victory and beheld men and women responding to the influence and sway of the gospel which they preached, they rejoiced greatly that the spirit of Christ was at work among them. The common feeling tone of life makes people of different backgrounds and walks of life one in attitudes and actions. People who have shared common sorrows and joys are often drawn to each other unconsciously.

Some years ago in a parish in Omaha, Nebraska it was my responsibility as pastor to conduct a service of comfort for a family whose infant had been snatched from them. This was a community in which there was much tension and hostility due to racial bitterness, but a member of another racial group came in and sat through the entire service. At times she seemed tense and her face reddened with deep concern. In the closing moments of the service the grief-stricken mother was allowed to stand by the side of the casket and take a last look at the sacred remains of her departed child. The visitor from the other race walked to the casket and, placing her arms around the waist of the weeping mother, joined her in tears of grief.

When the services were completed we were curious to know what had brought this visitor. Upon inquiry we learned that just a few days before she had also laid her own departed child to rest, and that common experience of grief rose above sectional prejudice and united the souls of two mothers in a common fellowship. The common sorrows among the believers in Christ have always united their hearts under the shadow of the Cross of Him who was Himself acquainted with grief.

It is true that some of the highest achievements of the Christian church have come in times of stress. Out of the dark ages came the testimony of heroic sons of light. In periods of oppression, great statesmen and national heroes came forward to defend the rights of the less fortunate and in ages of persecution prophetic spirits and saintly souls joined together in testimony for the Kingdom of God. But these positive results are not offspring of the forces of division and destruction. Rather these positive fruits are due to the fact that the constructive and the creative were the common denominators in spite of the presence of the negative.

Great religious leaders have appeared in desert places, proclaiming their prophetic messages of moral revolution and religious revival only because they have been able to see and comprehend the Kingdom of God. When the church through its ministry and gospel has summoned the guilty to a renewal of life, it has not been only to insure that they escape the wrath of God that was soon to come, but because they had been inspired and impelled by the vision of the Kingdom of God at hand.

In every country there are symbols and accepted standards which serve as the embodiment of the life, spirit, and soul of the nation. The sight of these stir deep emotions of love and respect for the country in every loyal citizen. The country's flag becomes the symbol of the nation's life and it is always treated with tender reverence. With the flag, soldiers are led to battle to suffer and die for the sake of their native land. Every country has a national anthem that becomes the voice of the nation. When it is sung, souls are stirred and the hearts of citizens are lost in patriotic ecstasy. In this music the harmony of the nation's life flows like a rippling stream and its spirit shines as the morning sun.

In such atmosphere disloyal people and traitors are not at ease and cannot long endure for they are driven by the expulsive power of a national affection while those who love their country are drawn closer to one another and to the nation's life.

All discords are lost in this patriotic hymn; all differences are subdued and dissolved in the warmth of the national spirit, and self interest is submerged in the broader concern for the country's life and destiny. It is not the individuals' life but the life of the nation that counts. At such a high moment citizens do not seek rewards for themselves but delight in giving their all even to the surrender of their own life's blood for the security of the nation.

The Christian church has her symbols and hymns of praise that mellow the minds and hold in deepest loyalty the souls of all who believe. The Cross, the symbol of the church, tells of the divine concern for all the children of men and points the way to a common Father and a lofty destiny. Christians sing not simply of the nation's life but of the glory of the Kingdom of God which is broader than country. Believers march together under the one banner of Jesus Christ and lose themselves in the eternal fellowship of the spirit.

With their agreements Christians can be and are drawn closer together and made into the image of the dynamic community of Jesus with the strength and potentiality of the promised Kingdom of righteousness and truth that shall stand as a living, growing, and redemptive fellowship of Jesus Christ. These undisputed agreements are the forces which can conquer all divisions, heal breaches of the past, and permeate the world Christian community with contagious goodwill, the love of God, and the peace of Christ. This will season the soul of all believers like salt, transforming all relationships with the yeast of divine grace which is hidden in the measured meal of humanity.

10

THE URGENCY OF CHRISTIAN FELLOWSHIP

WE HAVE TAKEN the position that the matters on which there is inescapable agreement are most fundamental to the life of the Christian church, and through their agency a world Christian fellowship can be constructed. The call to harmonize these agreements in the interest of such a fellowship does not in any wise underestimate the influence of obvious existing differences. When we say that these agreements include some of the fundamentals of the Christian religion we do not mean that differences are surface. It is true that they may appear to be surface when compared to the great themes of the eternal gospel of Christ, but these differences are by no means superficial.

The matters that have divided the Christian church regard interpretations of the meaning of the gospel: the dogmas of the church. Here are problems that are hard to solve. They are made more difficult because of the long history behind them and the attitudes and emotional patterns that have been developed in their regard. It is not easy to modify or re-vamp a dogma; it is not easy to change some ancient theological position without the danger of doing injury to delicate fibers of one's faith. The roots and tendrils of one's doctrine entwine themselves about the object of one's faith as a growth on the brain wraps its roots around the delicate tissues thereof. Only the skilled hands of a trained surgeon can perform an operation to remove such brain growth without damaging this central organ of the nervous system.

Roman Catholic, Orthodox, and Protestant theologians have admitted that the problems of Christian unity are basically problems of doctrine. And changes at this point are not easily made. When they are attempted it requires the genius of our best theologians. In my first visit with Pope John XXIII, he said that one of the problems of Christian unity revolves around doctrine. He re-emphasized the same basic idea in his opening address at the Second Vatican Council.

Dr. Karl Barth emphasized the seriousness of this problem when stating his position on a proposed conversation between Protestant and Roman Catholic theologians. Dr. Barth said:

If one should dare to enter into such a conversation . . . and if it is to be meaningful, then it should concern itself with a serious question, i.e., with a question of dogmatics and precisely with this question which, if all signs do not mislead, is the very touchstone of spiritual division. This should be done even though at the very most the result of this conversation can be no other than that we come to agree why and in what respect as matters stand now we cannot come to an agreement.[1]

It is clear to students of Christian unity that the walls which separate Catholics and Protestants are not ultimately historical or sociological, but theological. To begin with these great differences in our quest for unity of believers requires that the theological problems be solved first and this in turn requires the work of specialists. Many years of success and failure are necessary before the desired unity can be achieved. This road is a long and hard one. It is too much to expect the human mind to respond to the power of argument, the logic of reason, and the

[1] Callahan, Daniel J., *et al.*, eds., *Christianity Divided: Protestant and Roman Catholic Theological Issues* (New York, Sheed & Ward, 1961), p. 153.

impact of moral persuasion which involve giving up set theological beliefs for the sake of a new and improved Christian togetherness. It would involve the surrender of old values because new ones are better.

The human mind is so constructed that it is not able to surrender cherished values simply because they are criticized or opposed. Here compromise is most difficult even if one were willing to accept it. The task of unlearning what one has learned, of giving up things on which one has relied, is almost beyond the reach of the average mind especially when the things involved are concerned with issues of eternal salvation or everlasting punishment.

As important as the theological problem must be, it is not this writer's position that we must begin here, or nowhere, in order to move toward the fulfillment of the prayer of Jesus that "they all might be one." When we begin with accepted agreements and build a fellowship on them, we have made a most vital step. This is a step that can and ought to be made not only by theologians and denominational leaders, but by the rank and file of believers the world over. The call here is not to surrender any values but to employ values that God has given to the Christian church as a whole in the interest of the development of a world Christian fellowship. Since the basic things on which all Christians agree are the very heart of the Christian gospel, a fellowship built on them is by no means superficial but realistic and enduring.

In a fellowship there need not be sameness. Organic union is not the immediate goal of our striving, but a togetherness that acknowledges differences but also recognizes the existence of a vital kinship that may be used right now in the service of our God. In the future, this may result in organic union or another constructive form of togetherness. But right now our concern is the full realization of the fellowship.

A Christian world fellowship is a most urgent need of the hour. It is also a present possibility and an emerging reality.

Divisions among believers have already taken too great a toll. Now is the time to begin in earnest, building and harnessing a world Christian fellowship for the weal of man and the glory of God. The call is urgent. The need is great. And the hour has come. A call to fellowship is not a call from the more difficult to the less difficult. It is a call to the most vital, the most constructive and the most creative venture for the Christian church in this hour.

A fellowship is the most urgent need for the church within herself. In this context the church seizes the values that are not available to her and resolves to live in peace in spite of problems not yet solved. Here she accepts the incoming tide of the Holy Spirit and sails on its crest out upon the wide seas of divine providence trusting God for the future that lies ahead. Jesus Himself ascribed great power to a fellowship of believers, however small. Such power is urgently needed in the church today. In the first place, Jesus taught that a prayer of a fellowship could compel a ready response from the Father in Heaven. Said He:

. . . I say unto you, that if two of you shall agree on earth as touching anything that they shall ask it shall be done for them of my father which is in heaven (Matthew 18:19).

God will work with and through the smallest possible fellowship. Jesus says "if two of you shall agree." He could not reduce the size of the fellowship to a smaller number, for less than two would be no fellowship at all. It is not then the size that is significant but the agreement. If they agree and then make their request of God He will hear their petition, but He requires them to begin at a point of agreement. For where a few come together on earth in agreement on things of the spirit, God will hear their prayers and grant their request. Humble people of the lowly earth in a fellowship of agreement may summon blessings from the heavenly plains and claim the aid of God Himself.

But what if they do not agree? What if they meet to debate some problem of theology or to wrestle with some issue of philosophy? And what if they have present with them some of the greatest thinkers? And what if their meeting is fraught with conflict? The answer is clear. There will not be the promised divine visitation. A ritual of prayer is useless without a fellowship of agreement. Our differences are a barrier in reaching the throne of God in prayer.

The church needs now, and has needed in the past, more of a power of God and a life of the spirit. All of this is available if the approach is made through a fellowship of agreement. The church can afford to lose an argument if in so doing she wins new vantage in the Kingdom of God. She may also lose the certainty of a past philosophical interpretation of life if in so doing she gains a meaningful fellowship and earns the right to make her request known to God. The prayer life of the church is most essential and *now is the time* to remove every roadblock to its success.

God will not withhold His blessings from the church if she will approach Him in the right way. He is ready before the church speaks and has the plan for her life before she prays, but He cannot reach her when she destroys the possibility of a fellowship by confusion and conflict. Divisions are poor conductors of the Spirit; disagreements always impede the work of the Divine. The Holy Spirit worked miracles in the early church when that group represented a fellowship held together by agreement. When they prayed, God heard their prayer.

In the next place Jesus teaches that a Christian fellowship meeting in His name is an invitation to Him to be present with them. Said He:

For where two or three are gathered together in my name, there am I in the midst of them (Matthew 18:20).

He is positive on this point: if they meet in His name, He is there. He does not promise His presence in a fellowship that is called together in any other name. It is possible to meet in the name of philosophy, in the name of business, in the name of accepted traditions of a people, or in the name of a thousand other things, but if we do not meet in the name of Jesus, He is not there.

The small fellowship that Jesus speaks of may comprise as many nationalities and races as there are people present, and their intellectual outlook on life and their economic possessions may be as varied as their cultural backgrounds, but if they meet in His name, this one fact democratizes their differences, and renders them a company in which He delights to dwell. The primary struggle of the church should be to keep the name of Jesus, that is, His authority, His purpose, and His directives in the center of their thoughts, desires, and actions. In the quest for growth and development the church should never leave out the name of Jesus. In taking His name we take Him, His message, His power, and His way of life.

The gospel of Jesus Christ must not be diluted to meet the approbation of modern man. Its claims must not be reduced to the level of the worldly crowd, and its demands must never be lowered to gain the approval of those who find Jesus the Christ too stern to be endured, and His Cross too hard to bear. The gospel of Christ must not be too much mixed with Aristotle and Plato, for in such a mixture the genius of the Son of God will not shine forth as God's beam of everlasting grace. The name of Jesus Christ must always remain at the center of our Christian fellowship. For if His presence go not with us we are lost in the modern wilderness of make-believe and are helpless in the great struggle for world redemption.

People in foreign fields have in the past rejected western culture and repudiated that missionary program which concerned itself more with the economic expansion of the sending country than the betterment of the people to whom it ministered. But all over the world men and nations have listened with rapt attention to the gospel story and have welcomed the message of salvation brought in the name of Jesus Christ. They have sought and found in Him a friend and a Savior.

The presence of Jesus Christ can work miracles among men. He can harness human resources and the noble gifts of society for the advancement of the Kingdom of God. Jesus Christ can use the pageantry, ritual, and drama of the Roman Catholic Church to aid in the work of His Kingdom. He can speak through the silence of Quakers. The music and message of Protestant churches can be used to help evangelize the world and save the lost.

Pentecost is another story of what happens to a fellowship when it is dominated by the Divine Presence. God works in the fullness of time. When the Day of Pentecost was fully come they were all with one accord in one place (Acts 2:1). Here was the fellowship that had prayed for and expected the Divine Visitation. If these apostles had set out on their respective tasks before the Day of Pentecost their messages might have become a series of varied and confusing stories that doubtless would have advanced their respective notions, but would have negated and possibly refuted the kingdom message of Jesus Christ. But they obeyed their Master and waited in His name for the coming of the Divine Presence, and by so waiting they received the gift of the Holy Spirit.

This early fellowship met the challenge of the divine hour. Here was a ready field for the spread of the Holy Spirit. They were in one accord. One accord is God's chord on which He can play the music of eternity and from which can radiate the truths, riches, and glory of His promised kingdom. One accord is that live wire over which may come the divine current from the heavenly fields which may purge the heart of sin and quicken the souls to new life, new insights, and new powers. They were all with one accord in one place and God met them with the fulfillment of the promises of Jesus Christ. The weak received strength, the church a guide, and the preacher a comforter with courage. Thus started the church of Jesus Christ on its long mission of cross-bearing and redemption.

What are the blessings of the spirit that await us? What are the new depths of insights that remain for the people of God? And how far removed is that day when God shall rescue the present social order from the hands of blood-thirsty men and the throes of godless tyrants? How near is the end of oppression and when is the reign of justice, goodwill and peace? When will nations begin to junk their stockpiles of destruction and turn their armaments into tools for cultivation and machinery for production? The positive answers to these searching questions lie not with statesmen who are greedy for power and filled with the lust for other lands but with the church of Jesus Christ which is the community of the redeemed. When we plant ourselves on that solid foundation laid by Jesus Christ and become a people of one accord—though scattered throughout all the earth—the Spirit of God will move upon us, the breath of goodwill revitalize us, and we will be moved to testify to the saving power of the grace of God. And men will not ask in what denominational family did you first meet the Christ but will ask only if you are among those who know Jesus Christ as the Revealer of God and the Savior of all mankind.

This age is aware of the fact that its great need is for constructive and creative human relations. As we review the tragic results of two world wars in the last two generations and observe the frantic preparations that men and nations are now making for another possible conflict, we are not only aware of the tragic waste in human material, the horrible crimes against human personality, and the acts of oppression and slavery, but we are also impressed again with the tremendous need for the knowledge and practice of the highest type of human relations. At this point the church owes the world a tremendous debt. The greatest possible social miracle that could take place today would be for mankind to find and actually practice the relationships that would not only protect and preserve the right intellectual, moral and spiritual values from the past but would teach men how to inspire other human beings in the practice of those human relationships.

Although it is convinced of the need for peace, the world has not learned as yet how to secure, preserve and practice it in the normal relationships of nations to nations and peoples to peoples. Whatever system of thought or economic program that is able to guide man in the much needed and much desired relationship referred to above will become world-wide, world-respected and universally accepted. This will be true whether the program comes from the hands of atheistic and materialistic men or from political systems that guarantee the economic well-being of all citizens and the liberation of the oppressed from their chains and from the thralldom of their oppressors.

Interestingly enough, the appeal of international communism to the oppressed, the dispossessed, the lonely and the poor of the earth is not an appeal based upon the intricate philosophies of Karl Marx, Friedrich Engels, or Nikolai Lenin. The average man cannot comprehend fully the Communist Manifesto of 1848, but he can understand the promises and, in some measure, the practices which give relief to the poor and possessions to the dispossessed. This understanding endows them with a conviction, whether true or false, that they are the benefactors of a way of life which renders to every man his just desserts in the struggle of life.

When Adolph Hitler came to power in Germany and embarked on his dogma of the superior race with a political philosophy and military system to back up his program, few of the German people fully understood the long-range effects this would have on the life and destiny of their beloved fatherland. They were captivated by Hitler's promises of victory and overcome by the anticipation of revenge for their nation for the defeat of the First World War. They saw themselves lifted out of an economic depression, freed from world political oppression and made once again a free people enjoying all the privileges of a noble race. But the venture was wrong and the nation went down to defeat.

People of the earth today cry for deliverance from their chains and freedom from those forces that would curse and kill. They are hungry for the true bread of life and that water that satisfies their deepest thirst. Men in the prison of their divisions have learned through conflict, suffering, and defeat that they need a new type of relationship, a new type of creative togetherness that will recognize the rights of men and will administer to their deepest needs.

If it would find men and nations where they are most in need and show them the way that they long have sought, the church today must begin at that focal point where man is related to man, brother to brother, nation to nation, and mankind to God. But before the Christian church can minister to the needs of a confused, divided, and hostile world, the church must overcome its own sins of division. When the church would address herself to the task of peace, world brotherhood, the advancement of justice, equality, righteousness, and truth, history points an accusing finger and shouts defiantly this sad warning to her: "Would be physician heal thyself, emancipator break thy chains and make thine own fetters fall." The surest way for the church to effectively espouse the cause of world brotherhood and the cause of an enduring and lasting peace is for her to practice Christian fellowship within her own ranks and to adhere to a constructive and creative harmony in spite of her differences.

The need for Christian fellowship is *now*. Hostility, strife, and religious prejudices are luxuries that the church cannot afford. The question confronting mankind is not necessarily how to analyze philosophical problems or how to explain dogmas of theology, but how to live together in a fellowship that is both constructive and creative.

Modern man is struggling to build a world fellowship that will transcend national and racial barriers and result in a community of goodwill and peace where war as a means of settling national and international disputes will be a thing of the past. The nations tried this venture at the close of the First World War by organizing the League of Nations in April, 1919. This League endured for a period of twenty years and then it hit the rocks of international greed and power, floundered and went down. The nations were in earnest but they were too much under the spell of the First World War to be able to chart an unbiased course for this new political experiment. Hands stained with blood of the past were too much in evidence and minds still wedded to the old colonial and imperial order were not able to erect a tabernacle of justice and peace that could survive the confusion of the times and subdue the lust for power.

A divided Christian church stood by and saw the League of Nations go down to defeat, a defeat that paved the way for a second world conflict that was worse than the first. Surely a body organized in the name of and under the banner of the Prince of Peace cannot escape much of the blame for the horrors of war and for the moral and spiritual climate in which warmongers are created and their diabolical plans for world destruction are born. But we must admit the church was so divided and so weakened by her devotion to the minor things of expediency that she did not have the vision, the moral strength, or the spiritual know-how to save the sinking ship and did not have enough divine power to administer the needed life to the dying past.

In 1945, a new attempt was made by the nations of the world to organize another international fellowship for peace. For eighteen years the United Nations has been struggling at her task. Much good has been done but she is not yet out of the danger zone. She is still rocking in the rough seas of international misunderstanding and conflict. If she is to survive the storm she needs the aid of some power that can help her. The nations of the world need help. This task belongs to the Christian church.

The nations need an example of a world-wide fellowship that will recognize all men as brothers united in one human family with a common destiny. The Christian church should be that example, but it cannot be divided into warring groups. Only as a united fellowship can the church become a blueprint for the desired peace of the world. The United Nations needs a message that can become the basis of a secure foundation on which to build a world community. The gospel of Jesus Christ is that story and the divine plan for universal salvation gives the meaning and moral dynamic that can aid the nations in their effort to merge the people of the world into one great fellowship of peace. This message tells how the spirit of love can lift all men above the lust for power without sacrificing the soul of their own nation or endangering the security of their people. The Christian church has had this message for two thousand years but has been handicapped in its proclamation because she had not been united in her testimony and has by her divisions negated the story that she is called upon to tell. The world fellowship of the church will give new credence to the message.

The United Nations needs today not simply the knowledge of the destruction that war can bring. She has this already, for history holds the memorials of every cursed conflict, and time has kept a record of the millions of casualties and the wreckage and the ruin that have been left in the bloodstained footsteps of the past. Today scientists have recited over and over again grim warnings of the destruction, death, and hell that will result from another conflict. Statesmen are not wanting in their desire to avoid war. This desire is in the hearts and minds of statesmen and is the hope of the nations, but they lack the power to win the peace they desire, and do not have the moral courage to go forth with all their might to achieve and to gain the peace they desire.

The Christian church has the power and the spirit for world peace. The power has been committed unto her. She has the spirit of truth, the redemptive influence of Christ, and the assurance that she has access to a rock of eternal security. But through her divisions she has been greatly weakened. A united fellowship is needed today to aid the church in extending a helping hand to the nations of the world where they need it most. The propaganda of war-mad statesmen, the power struggle of men of greed, the sound of every atomic blast, and the vision of the cloud formations tell us of the approaching day of gloom and of humanity's possible defeat and death. The church must not fail the nations and she must not fail her God. If she does not save the United Nations, the judgment of God shall fall upon her and she may lose her last chance to work for the Kingdom of God on this planet and in this generation.

11

ON THE ROAD TO A MORE COMPLETE CHRISTIAN FELLOWSHIP

IT IS NOW CLEAR that Christian world fellowship is an urgent need for the church herself and for the nations of the world. The dream is present and the vision is clear. The task is how to make this ideal a reality. There are some constructive things that we can do while differences still exist within the Christian family. There is only one way to take: the way set forth by Jesus Christ. This road may be viewed in the perspective of progressive phases through which the church must travel to reach the high standard for which Jesus prayed. There are at least four such stages to be considered in this chapter: tolerance, a better understanding, appreciation, and a fellowship of joint participation in some worthy task.

Each level should be pursued in light of the mutual understanding of the groups and according to their ability to participate in such an understanding. The degree of participation will depend on the scope of the points held in common. Attempts at fellowship should never be forced or overtaxing. Christian groups should not, for outside show, try to be and do more together than their experiences and accepted kinship will allow. For a fellowship program that strains present relationships and sends each group to a defensive position where each labors to protect and perpetuate its own traditions is more of a liability than an asset. Defensive attitudes soon precipitate fear, strife, and finally, open hostility. It is better to be separate and friends than to be together as potential or actual enemies. Just as external togetherness of Christian groups should always be inspired by a prior inner spiritual agreement, so the experience of kindred minds and fellowship of souls should always precede in time and experience the attempt at unification or merger of Christian denominations. It requires a strong spiritual fellowship to sustain the efforts at organic union among different Christian groups.

Already there are on record in the civil courts of our land sad stories of long, bitter, and costly legal battles between groups who have attempted to effect a merger of their denominations. Separation in peace is better than attempted mergers which not only result in conflict but also require the verdicts of the civil courts to resolve. When we seek first the life and power of the Spirit of God and that fellowship which grows out of the presence of the invisible Kingdom proclaimed by Jesus Christ, then all the necessary externals in life, including the growth of unity will be added. Christian fellowship should come first, and the future relationship between groups will be informed by that fellowship.

In the attempt to realize a more complete fellowship among the Christian families of the world, there will be—and in fact there must be—different levels of participation predicated upon the spiritual strength of the believers involved. Before a permanent superstructure of Christian unity can be erected and completed, we must painstakingly explore the sands of tradition until the firm and abiding rock of divine reality is reached. And what is built on this rock is permanent and secure, for the rock will not give way to pressure; it will not be moved by the winds of human opinion, nor washed away by the rains of conflict. What are some of these degrees of relationships now possible among believers? What segments on the way to deeper Christian fellowship must be traveled before the proposed day of better things shall arrive?

Divisions, schisms, feuds, and even open persecutions have marked the historical relationship of Christians with Christians.

Some who were of the same household of faith have even used the sword to send their neighbors to defeat and death. Wide and deep have been the chasms that have divided groups of professing Christians. These facts, however shameful and painful, cannot be denied. The evil work of centuries will not be corrected by human efforts in a short span of time. What the sword has wounded through the years will not be healed by the ointment of soothing words; what has been torn apart by the hatreds of men and the flames of persecution throughout centuries will not be restored by a few well-worded resolutions adopted in public assemblies. But if the breaches are to be healed, we must begin somewhere, knowing full well that the journey is a long and hard one.

The healthiness of a true, dynamic and creative Christian fellowship cannot come until the scars of the past are dealt with wisely and tenderly. The road to the desired fellowship is difficult. Every serious Christian knows this but he gives witness to his desire in spite of the difficulties. There must be a way that leads from where we are to where we ought to be. We must have the courage to find it and then set our faces like flint toward this high desire and pray that the Lord of life will make our feet like hind's feet for traveling the rough, stony road ahead.

The most elementary attitude that a person or group of persons should have toward people with whom they do not agree is the attitude of tolerance. Tolerance is the will to endure people who differ with us in opinion or belief. Tolerance is the will for co-existence with those who differ with our conception of religion or of life. When we reach the level of tolerance, a campaign of destruction is no longer needed. No longer is it considered a personal defect of character or a defeat of one's causes when that which is different is granted the same right to life, liberty, and the pursuit of happiness. Each continues to devote his time to the development of his tradition, seeking to develop to the highest possible degree the institutions he belongs to.

But when tolerance reigns, no time is lost living in the negative, working at the destruction of others. Now all are freed from the sin of bigotry, for each knows that there are others in the field of action beside themselves with rights, powers, and potentialities worthy of respect. This saves a person from thinking more highly of himself than he ought. In this frame of mind no one dares to think that his belief is the only belief and that he has all the rights of expression and of propaganda. Tolerance of others is the corrective for self-absorption.

Churches that are tolerant of others do not by this act compromise any of the principles of truth and righteousness that they hold dear, but they have simply accepted the fact that no church has all the knowledge about God. A chosen people of God is a people selected to perform a task at a given period in history. It does not mean that the blessings bestowed upon them by God exhausted the divine storehouse. God always has other blessings for other people. Intolerant believers act as if God needed them to help Him protect His Kingdom and to police the moral and spiritual order of the universe.

A great Hebrew scholar made an historic statement that revealed to his colleagues that it was not necessary for them to seek to arrest those who did not believe as they did, nor was it essential for them to serve as police officers to help God run the business of His Kingdom. It was his contention that there is a plan by which the wicked ones will come to naught, and there is a wideness in divine wisdom that makes certain the victory of all of those whom God has called. Gamaliel, a member of the Sanhedrin Council, a puritan among the religious order of his day and a doctor of law, had some valuable advice to give to the other members of the Council who sought to put an end to the work of the early disciples by putting them to death. When Gamaliel asked for an executive session of the Council, the apostles were dismissed. Then this great statesman spoke frankly to the members of the Council. Drawing on the records of history he recalled cases where men who set themselves up as deceivers of the people were in due course defeated by forces that they themselves could not control.

When they heard that, they were cut to the heart, and took counsel to slay them. Then stood there up one in the council, a Pharisee, named Gamaliel, a doctor of the law, had in reputation among all the people, and commanded to put the apostles forth a little space; And said unto them, Ye men of Israel, take heed to yourselves what ye intend to do as touching these men. For before these days rose up Theudas, boasting himself to be somebody; to whom a number of men, about four hundred, joined themselves: who was slain; and all, as many as obeyed him, were scattered, and brought to nought. After this man rose up Judas of Galilee in the days of the taxing, and drew away much people after him: he also perished; and all, even as many as obeyed him, were dispersed. And now I say unto you, Refrain from these men, and let them alone: for if this counsel or this work be of men, it will come to nought: But if it be of God, ye cannot overthrow it; lest haply ye be found even to fight against God (Acts 5:33-39).

What happened to Theudas and to Judas of Galilee is the common lot of all who trust in their own power! What is of man will come to naught. What is born of the will of dying men will of itself perish and be lost in the jaws of death. But what God builds no human hands can tear down and what He has purposed will surely come to pass though all the demons in hell should be arrayed against it. In tolerance, men not only learn that time will test human acts, but they learn a higher fact: whatever work is of God will stand and stand defiantly and he who seeks to overthrow it will draw God Himself as an opponent and win sure defeat as his reward.

In Christian fellowship we are not called to the odious task of sitting in judgment on the faith of another. Neither are we assigned the responsibiity of determining what church is right or what believer is of God, or what priest or bishop is commissioned by God. In an act of tolerance those things are left to the individual, to time and to the judgment of history and God. Christians in their respective traditions have received a call and they are heirs of a kingdom responsibility. They are to give their best in the service of their Christ. The supervision and the evaluation of their work is left to a higher power and is not the responsibility of those who are themselves engaged in the service of the Lord.

We must learn, if we do not already know, that we cannot make our hearts more clean by cursing others whose hearts are not clean. We do not come nearer to God by slaying those who have drifted from Him, but we draw near to our Lord when we in tenderness and love grant all men the right to approach God as they are led by Jesus Christ and to testify as they are inspired by the Holy Spirit. Grant every man the right to proclaim truth as he comprehends it and to preach the gospel of Christ as it is revealed to him. Such a spirit of tolerance will lay a firm foundation for a purer friendship among the believers of different religious traditions. At this point, seeds of Christian fellowship may be planted that will grow into a will for closer relations.

When shall one begin to find fault with one's brother? When shall we seek to correct those whose religious thoughts are different from ours? The answer is when our own thoughts and motives are pure, and when we have arrived at perfection. The counsel of Jesus is still relevant. Said He:

Why beholdest thou the mote that is in thy brother's eye, but considereth not the beam that is in thine own eye? (Matthew 7:3).

When we are tolerant, we recognize the fact that we are not in position to sit in judgment on others, for our wisdom is not wise enough, our perfection is not pure enough, and our strength is not strong enough for us to determine the value of another's faith.

In being tolerant we ascribe to others that which we desire for ourselves, namely, a freedom of religion which permits the choice of the means to serve God and the privilege to worship God according to the dictates of our consciences. This freedom not only grants to another the right to make wise choices but even the right to make unwise choices. Intolerance leads one to sin against the right of the freedom of choice. It takes from others the right to make their own decisions in matters of religion and aims at binding others to the thought-patterns of one's own orthodoxy. Here we experience conversion by force and not through inner conviction. Intolerance tends to destroy far more values than tolerance; for in the former we would destroy the faith, the good intentions, and the sacrificial service among those who differ with us; we would desecrate the values of charity, patience, and unselfish concern for the thoughts of others.

But tolerance is an atmosphere of spirit in which the greatest degree of freedom is granted to all peoples in matters of religious choices, and that freedom is the right of all people. Tolerance does not negate the right nor dispel the obligation of evangelism, nor does it preclude the right and the responsibility to propagate truth as one sees it. Tolerance does not encourage one to do the wrong but grants him the right to discover and choose the right. Tolerance admits that we are all imperfect and that our views are subject to error, and all of our righteous judgment may still be improved with the passing of time and with greater moments of inspiration. While we may not believe as another believes, we are obligated to ascribe to another the right to believe as he believes. But tolerance is just a beginning on the long road towards a more complete fellowship among believers.

In an attitude of tolerance among religious groups the requirements for membership are not compromised. Those who do not qualify as members of a particular denomination have the right to be members of the fellowship of those saved by the power of Jesus Christ. An historical example of this type of tolerance may be cited from the annals of the Roman Catholic Church. It has to do with that dogma which states that there is no salvation outside of the Church.

Leonard Feeney, an American priest, took this dogma and gave what the Church has since called a false interpretation to it. Feeney preached that apart from Catholics and their catechumens no man could possibly be saved.[1] This was a case of intolerance at its worst. Pope Pius XII corrected the misinterpretation of this dogma of the Roman Catholic Church by sending the famous Boston letter, dated August 8, 1949, to Cardinal Cushing of Boston. In this letter he gives the meaning of the dictum: "No salvation outside the Church." He points out that the statement is basically true but hastens to state that the interpretation of the statement is of such a nature that others outside of the official membership of the Roman Catholic Church may be included among the saved. He took the position that just as there is baptism of water so there is also the baptism of desire and that members who have the desire to be saved coupled with supernatural faith will be saved because in this respect they are members of the Roman Catholic Church by desire. In explaining this letter Gregory Baum makes this statement:

Belonging to the Apostolic community of believers is of equal necessity to salvation as the baptism by which we enter it. However, just as for baptism, so as regards Church membership, the merciful God who wishes all men to be saved grants under certain conditions the effects of salvation to the *desire*, effects which ordinarily are bestowed only on the *fact*. Just as there is a baptism of water and under certain conditions a baptism of desire, so there is a full membership in the Church (with the triple mark of baptism, creed, and communion) and under similar conditions a membership of desire. In the former case we speak

---

[1] Gregory Baum, O.S.A., *That They May Be One: A Study of Papal Doctrine* (Westminster, Maryland, The Newman Press, 1958), p. 29.

of belonging to the Church *in re,* in the latter of belonging to her *in voto.*[2]

Here there are two ways of becoming a member of the Roman Catholic Church; one is to be united to her in fact, and the other is to be in union with her by desire. The far-reaching interpretation of this historic doctrine of the Roman Catholic Church is a firm doctrinal basis for tolerance because it does not exclude Protestants or others who differ in creeds. It is clear and very explicit, however, that there are certain advantages and certain blessings that people may miss who do not take the three-fold steps: namely; baptism, creed and communion into the Roman Catholic Church, and the Church does not promise these blessings to members by desire, but she does confess that said members have access to the glories of the Kingdom, the riches of grace and the redemptive acts of the Cross of Christ. This illustration is not presented for the sake of analysis or judgment of any of the great doctrines of the Roman Catholic Church. It is used to exemplify a spirit of tolerance in the Roman Catholic Church. Similar illustrations can be found in the history of other religious groups among Protestants to establish this same principle of religious tolerance. Tolerance, then, opens the gate for friendship and for a better understanding among believers of varied theological positions.

If we are to continue the journey towards a higher degree of fellowship among Christian groups, we must go beyond tolerance to a better understanding of each other. This requires research and study. At this stage, we seek to become acquainted with what others believe and to understand why they have taken certain theological positions. Study and research are the best ways to break down the sins of misinformation, for out of misinformation often comes misrepresentation, and through misrepresentation may come prejudices and prejudgments. Many

[2] *Ibid.,* p. 30.

of us can recall how mistaken we were about others before we learned about the things for which they stood.

One of the tragedies of Christian division has been the biased judgments that have been advocated as facts. Many Protestants have heard only part of the story of the life and the achievements of the Roman Catholic Church. Too many of us in youth were taught the worst about this Church. Some Protestants have gone through the pages of history and have gathered reports of the evil deeds of corrupt men who were allied with the Roman Catholic Church. They have led others to believe that these evil deeds by some corrupt leaders were sanctioned by the Church at its best and were the standards by which the Church judged leaders as well as followers.

John Tetzell, a noted monk of Leipsig, Germany, because of his ability as a pulpit orator, was engaged by some Church authorities to preach in favor of indulgences in order to raise money for religious purposes. He was appointed as Inquisitor in 1516, when he published a design to grant indulgences to those who donated money to aid in constructing the Church of St. Peter in Rome. Tetzell's designs were opposed by Martin Luther who posted ninety-five theses on the door of the church at Wittenberg in which he pointed out the inconsistency in the practice of selling indulgences. This corrupt practice did not represent the normal standard of ethical judgments, and those like Tetzell who insisted on the sale of indulgences did not represent the pure stream of the spiritual life of the Church. In 1563, the Council of Trent reaffirmed that the Church has the power to grant indulgences but laid down the principle that indulgences are to be granted without price. This is an indication of a constructive and creative spirit within the Roman Catholic Church designed to correct the evils and to remove elements foreign to the spirit of charity and the divine purpose.

In the Roman Catholic Church, as in many other churches, there have been wicked men who made their way to high places and high-ranking leaders who were not loyal to the responsibilities entrusted to them. There have been some leaders who engaged in the work of persecution and the exploitation of the weak and in the grim business of denying to others freedom of religion. Those who have taught these things about the Roman Catholic Church have led some to believe that these men represented the heart of this Church. But this Church has not continued its mission of mercy because of, but in spite of those who have sinned against its high principles.

Those who taught us in youth these grim stories of the Roman Catholic Church did not take the time to tell us of the great saints and martyrs who gave their all for the cause of Christ. I, for one, had to learn by research of the contribution that Saint Francis of Assisi made not only to his Church but also to mankind. Here was a young man, an heir to wealth, with the right to live with honor on a legacy from his distinguished family. But being overcome by the spirit of the Humble Man of Nazareth, he renounced his wealth and rank, and wedded himself to poverty, spending the rest of his days as an apostle of love and a messenger of mercy.

Those who taught us in youth that the Roman Catholic Church was simply a replica of the ancient Roman Empire in its desire for power and wealth did not tell us the story of St. Thomas à Kempis who lived close enough to reality to discover the vision of God and whose brilliant mind has relayed to others the rich treasury of the Divine Life. He has left a series of meditations that are rich in things of the spirit and that come from the very heart of God. These rare gems can strengthen the soul of any human being who takes the time to meditate on them and to adopt them as principles of life. Many Protestants as well as Catholics have been strengthened and inspired by his book, *The Imitation of Christ*. The meditations of this book come to us fresh from the mystic soul of a great saint and from the heart of a devout follower of Jesus Christ.

Does it make us any less devout as Protestants to understand and to admit the contributions that the Roman Catholic Church has made to history and to society? Does it in any way pauperize our spirits to proclaim the rich heritage that has come down through the centuries from these Christian scholars and statesmen? Does it make us any the less messengers of Jesus Christ to admit that within the folds of the Roman Catholic Church have been thousands who have known the contemplative life, who have lived in cloistered monasteries in search of truth and in quest of God's will and way?

I have met some of the distinguished leaders in the Roman Catholic Church. In meeting Cardinal Cushing of Boston, Massachusetts, I met a courageous spirit, a man who has suffered much but who has dedicated himself to the service of his church. He has spent many days suffering, sometime in ill health, and yet with joy, and at times with strange humor, he has revealed to others what it means to live above religious prejudice and in the light of a fellowship that is inspired by the Christ of the Cross.

I also remember well my first meeting with the late Cardinal Stritch of Chicago. We struggled together for a constructive, Christian solution to some of the nagging problems of the city of Chicago. He approached these problems as a citizen and as a devout Christian whose deep concern was the welfare of human beings and the improvement of the quality of life within the city of Chicago.

My first meeting with Cardinal Bea in his private chambers at the Brazilian College in Rome was a rare opportunity and a moment of great inspiration. Here is a seasoned biblical scholar, a religious statesman who carries upon his stooped shoulders more than eighty years of labor, struggle, and sacrifice. And yet, he is radiant, full of joy, and gives one the impression of a victor in the battle of life. No wiser choice could have been made for President of the Secretariat for Promoting Christian Unity in the Second Vatican Council.

I cannot forget the great impression and the inspiration that came to me in my first personal and private audience with Pope

John XXIII, a man of deep convictions dedicated to the service of his Church and to his God, a lover of mankind. Pope John was the head of one of the largest Christian families in the world and yet he radiated a spirit of humility that was contagious and gave forth an atmosphere of goodwill and brotherhood. He met his fellowman as a brother and as a consecrated servant of God. What inspiration I would have missed if I had remained locked up in the prison of youthful prejudices and had looked on these distinguished religious statesmen as if they were less than their noble deeds and their dynamic personalities have revealed. What a tragedy it is that thousands of men and women in their contact with others are missing the pearls of great price, these rare gems of spiritual experience because they have elected to remain in fetters of prejudice, in chains of moral ignorance, and in spiritual bondage.

It is most encouraging that in recent years both the Roman Catholic and Protestant Churches have exchanged articles and statements on their respective theologies. In some cases they have written books jointly, setting forth their respective views in friendship and in brotherly love. These are signs of growing understanding between them.

To the Second Vatican Council which opened in St. Peter's Basilica in Rome, October 11, 1962, the Pope and the Church Fathers welcomed a group of Observers and Guests among them to listen to their deliberations. This was not forced upon them; it was done through their free and deliberate choice, as a part of their expression of goodwill and charity towards their Protestant brethren. On the 13th of October, 1962, Pope John XXIII held a private audience with Observers and Guests in his papal palace. He refused to sit upon his throne and chose rather to occupy a chair at the head of the circle. But before taking his seat he shook hands with each Observer and Guest personally, not by having them come to his chair, but by coming to them. After this rather informal greeting he made his address to us. Among other things he said:

Today's most welcome meeting is to be simple and freely respectful and brief. The first word which rises up in my heart is the prayer taken from the 67th Psalm. . . . In so far as it concerns my humble person, I would not like to claim any special inspiration. I content myself to the sound doctrine which teaches that everything cometh from God. In this sense I have considered this idea of the council which began on the 11th of October to be a heavenly inspiration. I confess to you that it was for me a day of great emotion.

On that providential and historic occasion I devoted all of my attention to my immediate duty of preserving my recollection of praying and giving thanks to God. But my eye from time to time ranging over the multitudes of sons and brethren and suddenly as my glance rested upon your group, on each of you personally I drew a special comfort from your presence.

Your welcome presence here and in the emotion of our priestly heart (the heart of the bishop of the church of God, as we said yesterday before the assembled council), the emotion of my beloved fellow-workers and, I am certain of it your own emotion too, combined to show you that there burns in my heart the intention of working and suffering to hasten the hour when for all men the prayer of Jesus at the Last Supper will have reached its fulfillment. . . . It is now for the Catholic Church to bend herself to her work with calmness and generosity; it is for you to observe her with renewed and friendly attention.[3]

These words and the fellowship of understanding enjoyed by us are experiences that can never be destroyed. We have met the Pope of Rome. We have met him as one who believed in God and who trusted in His providence and the guidance of His spirit. I shall long remember the impact of his personality, the warmth of his spirit, and the revelation of his deep concern for the welfare of not only the brothers within his own religious family, but also the brothers in other areas of the Christian fellowship and in other religious persuasions. Such an appreciation would have been impossible without an unprejudiced observation both of the man and his message.

[3] See text of Address in Appendix B, p. 186.

It is equally true that our Roman Catholic friends can recognize the presence and power of God in the lives of many dedicated Protestants. There are Catholics who have this awareness. Martin Luther and a company of other inspired reformers have made in their own way a distinct contribution to the cause of Christ. To this fact many Roman Catholic scholars and theologians have given their testimony.

Also there is a stream of inspired believers that is traced from the early apostles. They have always been in the minority but they too have given evidence of having been with the Christ and of learning His ways. These devout believers may be seen in the company of Mennonites and Waldenses and many other Christian minorities. A study of their courageous witness and of their suffering and even death for their faith tells us that they had been armed with the certainty of the presence and the power of Christ.

Time would fail us in an attempt to give the full story of the ministry of John Wesley and the devout life of John Knox who shook all Scotland with the fiery gospel that he preached. The history of the quest for freedom of religion would be far from complete without the heroic story of a Roger Williams wandering through the snow-filled swamps of Rhode Island seeking a refuge where it would be safe to preach the whole gospel of freedom to all the world. When we have told of the pulpit eloquence of the great Charles H. Spurgeon, Henry Ward Beecher, and George Trueitt the list would not be complete without some recognition of what God did with a slave boy in Richmond, Virginia in the conversion and the call to the ministry of old John Jasper. In this company appears that son of thunder, that unique and gifted preacher of the truth of Jesus Christ, C. T. Walker. A brief review of the sainted servants of God will teach people of all Christian groups how liberal God has been with His grace. In a spirit of intolerance, many precious sons of God are ignored.

In a spirit of intolerance much harm can be done not only

to religious groups but to large segments of God's human family. One of the tragedies of history is the sin of anti-semitism, an evil doctrine that has occasioned the suffering of millions of innocent people who are members of the Jewish religion. It is beyond reason and an evil practice of the most devastating and damnable kind when a person is found guilty for having been born into a particular group and thereby condemned. In the name of this prejudice, millions of innocent human beings have perished. The earth is poorer because of their suffering and death. Some of the basis for anti-semitism may be traced to a Christian interpretation of the relationship of the Jewish people both to Jesus Christ and to the Christian community. We have frequently heard the expressions, "the Jews were against Jesus," "the Jews killed Christ." Some feel hostility and resentment to Jewish people based on this particular emphasis and reference to Jewish attitude towards Jesus. We must admit that according to the records some of the outstanding opponents of Jesus were the religious leaders of His day, and most of these were members of the Jewish community.

But we have been too silent about the constructive contributions that have come to the Christian community from Jewish men and women. Not all Jews opposed Jesus Christ, not all Jews participated in the dreadful act of the Crucifixion, and not all Jews shouted for His condemnation and for His death. There were many Jews who followed Him, who accepted His truths, and who became the first disciples and early apostles of the Christian church. The Christian church began in a Jewish community and was comprised of members from that community. The New Testament is the first great book of the Christian church and the New Testament rests on the foundation of the Old Testament which was primarily a Jewish book. The work of God and the acts of the Holy Spirit as revealed and related in the Old Testament used Jewish men and women for the most part as the agents and the messengers.

No religious philosophers and no inspired prophets have surpassed the eighth century Hebrew prophets in their depth of insight, in their proclamations of a gospel of social justice and their optimism regarding the ultimate victory of righteousness over sin. The Jewish community has enriched the spiritual life of the world, and their genius has helped to plant the seeds of the on-going kingdom of truth in practically every nation under the heavens. It is indeed inspiring to note what a great contribution Jewish people have made to culture, civilization, and the upward progress of mankind. When they are understood in the light of history it will be discovered that they have survived persecution because of the power of the ideas they have embraced. In paying tribute to this great people, Max I. Dimont has said:

The furniture in the Western world is Grecian, but the house in which Western man dwells is Jewish. . . . The period of greatness of ancient Greece lasted five hundred years. Then that nation lapsed into a people of herdsmen, never again to regain its former glory. Not so with the Jews. Their creative period extends through their entire four-thousand-years of history. . . . From this people sprang Jesus Christ, acclaimed Son of God by more than eight hundred and fifty million Christians, the largest religious body in the world. From this people came Paul, organizer of the Christian church. The religion of the Jews influenced the Mohammed faith, second-largest religious organization in the world, with over four million adherents claiming descent from Abraham and Ishmael. The Mormons say they are descendants of the tribe of Israel.[4]

We have given this testimony at length so that doubters may investigate and seek the truth of a great people, and scholars may pause to reflect on the achievements of a people whose weapons have been creative ideas and whose God is the Lord. Much hatred would be removed from the modern world if men

[4] Max I. Dimont, *Jews, God and History* (New York, Simon & Schuster, 1962), pp. 11-18 *passim.*

tried to understand those whom they hate and were conversant with the values their opponents have conceived. To draw nearer to these great people with understanding, goodwill, and a recognition of our spiritual kinship does not in any way take from the Gentile world any of its blessings and natural gifts but tends to establish just reasons for the abolition of anti-semitism. The greatness of this people should be recognized and their place in history be given to them without prejudice and without fear.

Tolerance and understanding are vital steps but not the only steps in building a fraternity between those who have differences. At the third level, the level of the act of appreciation, one seeks to interpret values in the light of the meaning that these values hold for those who have adopted them. One tries to accept the meaning ascribed to these values without necessarily adopting them as one's own. It requires courageous, well-informed, and sensitive souls to appreciate the values of others. It is possible to know the genius in other people and yet be too fearful about one's own position to confess what the facts reveal. To put the proper estimate on the worth of others and to be fully aware of their qualities are indications of high achievement on the part of the objective observers themselves. Here the field of value is widened, and one becomes the heir of ideas, created by others. Appreciation of values in others need not cause any disregard for the sources of life that have produced and still sustain us. To admire the worth of others does not take from the values that we ourselves cherish.

When one stands with head bare in a reverent attitude while the people of another country salute their flag, he does not by such an act merit to be called a traitor. This is an act of appreciation. When one religious group respects the worship of another group, there is no compromise to his own values. One of the outstanding features of the World Council of Churches is the care with which they show their appreciation for the beliefs and worship of others. If one does not understand all that is done in the worship of others, it is important to know why it is done. This alone is the basis for respect.

Once in an assembly of Roman Catholics and Greek Orthodox, I saw the Roman Catholic cardinals and bishops stand as the officials of the Greek Church performed their rites. They were different from those of the Roman Catholic Church, to be sure, but by standing in respect the officials of the Roman Catholic Church ascribed to these rites the values proclaimed by the officials of the Greek Church.

Turning to the world of politics, one is aware that the philosophy of the east differs profoundly from that of the west. The communist conception of life in many ways is in contrast to the concepts of democratic nations. The cold war and the threats connected with it have not come about simply because of these differences, but because in many instances there is an attempt on the part of one group to depreciate the ideals of the other. An appreciation of the values of democracy on the part of the communist world and a like evaluation of communism on the part of the leaders in democracy would do much to bring about a more favorable climate for world peace.

It is natural for those who have been disrespected to rise to the defense of their rights and even to fight for those possessions that they hold dear. Granting people the right to be different without looking down upon them will tend to generate goodwill and peace.

The whole scheme of communication is based upon and is an act of appreciation. One need not be a trained artist to learn to appreciate what a painter has in mind with the strokes of his brush and the configuration of the paint upon his canvas. One need not know the technical rules of music in order to appreciate the story the musician tells in song. Differences there are, differences there will be, but they may be best approached in a spirit of appreciation.

A common task undertaken by different persons tends to draw them closer together. Where there is a common objective,

there is a tendency to employ similar means and to share antici-
pations, dreams, and efforts as the objective is approached. In
the early days of the modern ecumenical movement Protestant
church groups found themselves drawn closer together in the
common task of sending the gospel of Christ to peoples of other
lands. It was in this common missionary task that these churches
found less need for division and a more urgent demand for cooperation. As they sought to preach the gospel to the so-called
heathen nations, these churches found themselves facing a common enemy.

The answer to their common problems was the gospel of
Jesus Christ. Those who preach the same gospel while laboring
for the salvation of the lost will find a oneness of responsibility
that will result in the experience of a new spiritual kinship that
draws them closer together. There is today as great a need for
believers to engage in this common task as there was at the
very beginning of the Christian movement. The gospel of Jesus
Christ is and should be the central and the compelling task of
every church and every believer. Denominations may vary in
their organizational structures and their peculiar denominational
responsibilities, but these must always be made minor to the
major task of spreading the good news of the Kingdom of God.

After twenty centuries many changes have taken place; even
in the last few decades many peoples who were considered
primitive, heathen, and far-removed from the refinements of
western civilization are today moving forward as members of
the family of nations. Many of these peoples have joined hand
and heart with the historic leaders of western civilization and
hence can no longer be considered as heathen. These changes
of the times and the growth of nations will not allow western
churches to look down on the peoples of these new nations.
Some of the same short-comings among civilized people may be
found among so-called primitive people. Many of these new
nations have absorbed elements of our western culture and
have learned the sins and practices of modern man. Today the

dividing line between the saved and the unsaved can no longer be defined in terms of those that are heathen and those that are civilized. Often the most dangerous aspects of modern life may be found among the so-called civilized and advanced peoples. Today the lost are found in America, Europe, Asia, and on all the other continents of the world. For the first time in the history of civilization, man now possesses the power for complete, immediate self-destruction on a large scale. These new weapons can in a moment annilhilate western civilization and bring to doom and death the human race as we know it on this planet.

Every church that preaches a gospel of salvation must now be concerned about the primary task of saving man from himself if he is to be saved for the service of his Maker. The task at hand summons all the energy of the Christian church. If mankind is to escape the impending catastrophe, there must now be released the spiritual power that will cleanse men's souls of hate and draw them closer together in a fellowship of love and of peace. One need not be an expert in theology to see how essential it is that all believers the world over join together and work for the salvation of man from himself. This common task for understanding, social justice, world brotherhood, and peace is of sufficient depth, width, and breadth to summon the best there is in every church and in every denomination. The primary task at this point is not necessarily a common dogma or a common form of worship. First, it is most essential that we find and follow a common moral and spiritual task. And out of it shall come a new dynamic fellowship that shall hold different denominations and churches not only in the tender and constructive grasp of this ministry of world peace but also in the salvation of the nation.

It is clear then that all believers still have the common task of working for the advancement of the Kingdom of God and the salvation of all men. In this enlightened age our task is more than civilizing the so-called heathen. We must now save the so-called civilized from their heathen practices and purposes. Believers in different denominations are already committed to the dynamic, moral, and spiritual power that can redeem the individual life and also change human society from its destructive purposes and make it to become a creative force for good and for God.

With faith in God and utter commitment to Jesus Christ as Savior it is not too much to expect that believers the world over could meet periodically in a great world assembly and worship God and make plans for dramatizing the message of the Christians of the world. What has been done on a smaller scale can be done on a world-wide scale including all Christian groups. It is possible for men to pray to God in their own language and according to their respective traditions without calling into question the validity of their neighbor's approach. If the Spirit of God could work through different nationalities and languages on the Day of Pentecost such a dynamic Spirit could also work through the different methods, langauges, and religious practices of our people today. It could help unite our hearts in such a way that those who observe would know that we who have come together have been with Christ and that here is a fellowship of those who love Him. While there are many things on which believers still may differ, the things on which they agree are strong enough to keep before them the common task of making men into the image of the Christ and making society the beloved community of God.

IV

SOME ENCOURAGING SIGNS
OF THE TIMES

12

THE WORLD COUNCIL OF CHURCHES:
A CHRISTIAN FELLOWSHIP BY AGREEMENT

THERE IS STILL substantial work which remains to be done in the field of Christian unity before the prayer of Jesus, "That they may be one," shall become a living reality. There remain numerous problems to be solved, many haunting questions to be answered and different doctrinal rivers to cross before we reach the promised land of a world-wide Christian fellowship. Hence, much that we say now about such a fellowship must be placed in the category of visions that still tarry and desires still to be satisfied. But is it not better to dream of unity than to drift with complacency in the whirling floods of bitter partisan religious warfare? And is it not wiser to grasp the idea of a world-wide Christian fellowship than to perish in the valley of divisions?

There are already in existence some historic achievements of Christian unity and of fellowship in action. To have spoken on existing Christian agreements and the possibilities of a world-wide Christian fellowship based on them might have seemed abstract and too fantastic prior to 1948. But 1948 marked the official beginning of what is now known as the World Council of Churches. For the past fourteen years this organization has been a vital Christian fellowship influencing the lives of believers around the world. Although it does not represent the end of the struggle, the World Council of Churches is a concrete illustration of what is taking place among Christians of the modern world in the quest for fellowship and unity.

What is the World Council of Churches? The question can best be answered by beginning with a brief statement of what it is not. The World Council of Churches is not a super-church designed to negate and to control the thought patterns of its member churches. The World Council makes no demands upon any of its constituent bodies that would tempt or force them to acts of disloyalty to their own cherished traditions. It has not and does not require the surrender of any of the doctrinal positions of its member churches. It assumes no authority over the minds and souls of its constituents. These member bodies are as free to carry on their respective denominational programs after taking membership in the World Council as they were before. The World Council is not a rigid religious body politic seeking by its authority and power to develop doctrinal sameness. Speaking of the World Council and its authority, Archbishop Temple once uttered these memorable words:

It is not a federation as commonly understood, and its assembly and a central committee will have no constitutional authority whatever over its constituent churches. Any authority that it may have will consist in the weight it carries with the churches by its wisdom.[1]

Furthermore, the World Council of Churches is not a nationalistic organization designed to serve the cause of any single nation. It is not the voice of the West against the East, nor is it the testimony of the East against the West. Since it is not dominated by any particular economic or political philosophy, its members are drawn from every continent on the globe, from the East and West.

What then is the World Council of Churches? It is a fellowship of churches confessing the lordship of Jesus Christ and seeking to work out its destiny in the light of this abiding faith. Until 1961 the basis for the World Council read as follows:

[1] Rouse, Ruth, et al., eds., A History of The Ecumenical Movement (Philadelphia, The Westminster Press, 1954), p. 704.

The World Council of Churches is a fellowship of churches which accepts our Lord Jesus Christ as God and Savior.

Nothing more was required of churches than an affirmation of this position. In New Delhi the basis of the World Council of Churches was changed by a vote of 383 to 36, with 7 abstaining. Today the basis of the Council is stated as follows:

The World Council of Churches is a fellowship of churches which confesses the Lord Jesus Christ as God and Savior according to the Scriptures and therefore seeks to fulfill together their common calling to the glory of the one God, Father, Son and Holy Spirit.[2]

It is important to note that the Council is a fellowship comprising churches that differ greatly in forms of worship and in doctrine, but they have found their common ground in the Lord Jesus Christ as God and Savior. They have accepted as their common calling the propagation of the truths of the gospel of Christ and the advancement of the blessed community as proclaimed by Jesus. This fellowship is held together by a common faith in one God, one Savior who is our redeeming Christ, and one Holy Spirit that moves upon the hearts of all believers.

Christian unity today as reflected in the World Council of Churches is more than an unanswered prayer. It is more than the unfulfilled dreams of Christian statesmen and devout saints of ages past. In the World Council of Churches, Christian fellowship is now deeper than the speculation of theologians and higher than the intentions of kingdom-minded denominational leaders. Christian unity and Christian fellowship have in the last half century come to a new fruition and achieved new goals, and there are now recorded facts that give unquestioned testimony to the existence and power of a new Christian to-

2 Visser 't Hooft, W. A., Editor, *The New Delhi Report: The Third Assembly of the World Council of Churches* (New York, Associated Press, 1962), p. 426.

getherness that is world-wide in scope. We know it is not a
perfect achievement, but it is an achievement. It is not complete
in its growth, but its growth is both progressive and vital. This
world Christian fellowship is built on the basic and vital content
of the Christian religion. It stands on that rock upon which Jesus
promised to build His church. For that reason it is believed
that the gates of hell shall not prevail against this world-circling
fellowship.

The World Council of Churches was not hurriedly thrown
together by the vote of a few conscientious religious leaders. A
study of this fellowship reveals not only how thorough was the
planning but also how thoughtful and prayerful were the actions.
The tender roots of this precious plant extend far back into
the historic desires, sincere efforts, and prayers of believers for
a closer fellowship in Christ. Many Christian denominations in
their competitive struggles on the mission fields were shocked
to discover how much was lost through duplications, conflicts,
and competition. The type of common problems that they encountered on foreign fields reminded them of the kinship of
their struggles and drove them to a keen awareness of their
common purposes under God. In spite of their respective
denominations these believers had gone out to preach the same
gospel in the name of the same God and by the authority of
the same Christ and under the guidance of the same Holy
Spirit. Consequently it was in the throes of the great missionary
passion and struggle that the modern ecumenical spirit was
born and out of which has come a world-wide Christian fellowship.

If the nineteenth century marks the historic period in the
Christian church when denominational divisions reached their
highest peak, one can rejoice in the fact that the first half of
the twentieth century can be remembered as the period of the
greatest progress toward a world-wide fellowship among believers since the church was first commissioned. But even in
the nineteenth century there was the stirring of a spirit aimed

at the achievement of greater unity. It was William Carey, one of the great missionary spirits, who proposed a conference in Capetown, South Africa, in 1810 that would bring together all councils, organizations, and groups to deal with the problem of unity and cooperation. This meeting never took place, but somehow the vision did not die.

One hundred years later there was a great missionary conference called in Edinburgh that became the fountainhead of other missionary councils and conferences, forerunners of the World Council of Churches. The World Missionary Conference at Edinburgh in 1910 is one of the great landmarks in the modern ecumenical movement. These people were drawn together in the interest of understanding and cooperation. They sought to deal with things on which they could find agreement. They did not wrestle with problems of theological differences, neither did they seek to solve problems that would have strained or possibly broken the budding fellowship that they did enjoy.

At this Conference both the older and the younger churches were present. The younger churches, afflicted with many divisions among themselves, soon realized that they needed to stand together in order to avoid the danger of perishing separately. The forces of their native culture and the constant opposition from other religions led the members of the younger churches to go in quest of a togetherness that cut across denominational lines and rose above surface differences. Although representatives from the younger churches were few in number, about seven to be exact, they gave their testimony and influence regarding the need and the importance of this type of fellowship.

At the Edinburgh meeting not all of the members present desired to avoid facing the problems of differences. It was Bishop Charles H. Brent who took a firm stand for confronting the problems of Faith and Order on which there were great differences. But such a conference was not assembled until seventeen years later when the first Conference on Faith and Order met at Lausanne, Switzerland. Yet out of the findings and influence of Edinburgh came the desire for the church to become more involved in the problems of man's struggle with man.

Four years after Edinburgh the devastating calamity of World War I fell upon the civilized world. The representatives of the church of Jesus Christ felt a need to rally the forces that they represented to help save man from himself. It was Archbishop Nathan Soderblom who led the forces into the historic meeting at Stockholm, Sweden, in 1925, and here the first World Conference of Life and Work was organized. With the coming of the World Council of Faith and Order two years later in the historic Lausanne Conference, the church then had experienced two aspects of Christian unity or fellowship. Life and Work specialized in the application of the message of the church to the problems that confronted both the church and the nations of the world. The common task of salvation was enough to summon all believers to work together. The Faith and Order movement concerned itself with the elimination of differences and the achievement of basic and constructive agreements.

In 1937 these two world conferences met, Life and Work at Oxford University, and Faith and Order at Edinburgh University. The growing spirit of fellowship moved the statesmen and delegates to make an attempt to merge these two separate branches of the ecumenical movement. It was voted that in the next session Faith and Order and Life and Work would not meet as separate councils but would come together and form a World Council of Churches.

After much labor and study, prayer and sacrifice, a historic event took place in Niewe Kerk at Amsterdam, Holland, August 23, 1948. Here 147 churches from 44 countries representing 351 official delegates adopted the resolution that resulted in the formation of the World Council of Churches. Few can ever forget the atmosphere and the rich spiritual experience of that sacred hour. After the report was read by Dr. March Boegner of France and after the adoption of it, there was a meaningful

moment of silent prayer after which the Archbishop of Canterbury led a public prayer that shall live as long as the story of
Christian fellowship is told and retold by the believers in Christ.

Almighty God, here we offer unto Thee our thanksgiving and praise,
that Thou has brought us to this hour and this act in the faith of
Christ and by the power of the Holy Spirit. As Thou hast prospered
those into whose labours we enter, so, we pray Thee, prosper us in
this our undertaking by Thy most gracious favour, that in all our
works begun, continued and ended in Thee we may set forth Thy
glory for the well-being of Thy Holy Church and the salvation of all
Thy people.[3]

This achievement was due to careful planning, study, understanding, tolerance, and appreciation of the points of views of
others. Amsterdam was also the result of the work of the Holy
Spirit in the hearts of men. I was greatly impressed with the
humble statement made by a young Dutch boy who was
assisting delegates with their luggage. As he looked at people
from different sections of the world, speaking different languages, dressed in different costumes, he said: "People from
all over the world are coming to Amsterdam, and just think,
Jesus Christ brings them here!"

Since that historic occasion the fellowship has kept its promise
made in these words: "We intend to stay together." Since that
day there have been two other world assemblies of the Council.
One at Northwestern University (Evanston, Illinois) in 1954
and another in New Delhi, India, in 1961. At the Third World
Assembly in New Delhi, India, there were 176 member churches
representing Protestants, Anglicans, Orthodox and Old Catholic
communions from 52 different countries. In this meeting 23 new
churches were added, most of them coming from the younger
churches. Among these were also representatives from the
Russian Orthodox Church.

[3] Rouse, Ruth, *et al.*, eds., *op. cit.*, p. 720.

Not only in numbers but also in spirit of love and understanding, the World Council of Churches is still a growing fellowship. It now includes all major Christian bodies with the
exception of the great Roman Catholic Church. Let critics say
what they will and let doubts accumulate, we cannot avoid the
fact of the existence of this world fellowship of believers. Its
moral and spiritual impact and its mission for world peace
must not be taken lightly, for God is at work in such a fellowship.

On the front cover of the *Philippine Christian Advance and
Rural Fellowship Bulletin* (November, 1961) Mr. Solomon A.
Saprid, the art editor, has told a great story with an illustration.
The picture includes the official seal of the World Council of
Churches which is a boat with a cross serving as its mast. The
artist has the cross standing on a raft of logs; each log repre-
sents a church added to the council.

The more logs strongly tied together on the raft the more is its
capacity to carry load and to withstand the beatings of the waves of
the raging sea. On the raft are two men symbolizing mankind. Mankind
could only be brought to the haven of rest and peace on the Oikumene
raft where the cross or the Spirit of Christ is made central in the life
of the churches.[4]

The third meeting of the Assembly of the World Council of
Churches in New Delhi, India in 1961, impressed upon the
world that this fellowship is still moving forward in spite of the
turbulent seas in which it sails. And it is gathering strength as
it sails. Christian unity becomes a more vital hope because of
its growing strength. The success of this voyage will determine
in large measure the future of mankind. Nicholas Zernov says:

[4] "The Third Assembly of the World Council of Churches," *Philippine
Christian Advance & Rural Fellowship Bulletin*, XIII (November, 1961),
p. 3.

The future of mankind depends on the restoration of Christian unity and the reconciliation of Eastern and Western Christians is the pivot on which the success of this task depends.[5]

The World Council of Churches, although only fourteen years old, speaks to us out of the past and seems to point to a brighter day for Christian togetherness. The threat of atomic destruction is still with us and angry statesmen still rattle their modern spears of destruction. But the World Council of Churches is dramatic testimony that the soldiers of the Cross are also on the march. Christ and His host will not give up the struggle for the Kingdom of love and peace until the reign of God is established on every continent and its influence spans the seven seas and reaches from pole to pole.

[5] Rouse, Ruth, *op. cit.*, p. 674.

13

THE ROMAN CATHOLIC CHURCH AND THE ECUMENICAL SPIRIT

THE ROMAN CATHOLIC CHURCH is not a member of the World Council of Churches; it did not officially send Observers to either one of the first two world assemblies. However, the fact that the Roman Catholic Church has not taken an active part in the deliberations of the World Council does not mean that the Church is uninterested in furthering a world Christian fellowship. Five Observers were sent to the Third World Assembly at New Delhi in 1961 and were cordially received. An unprejudiced look at the Roman Catholic Church which observes some of its expressions and actions reveals that there is at work among her leaders a strong ecumenical spirit. This spirit has expressed itself in matters far more significant than the sending of Observers to the Third World Assembly. The greatest testimony comes to us from the Second Vatican Council that was convened in Rome under Pope John XXIII, October 11, 1962.

Prior to the convening of the Second Vatican Council many discussions between Roman Catholic and Protestant theologians had taken place. These scholars had openly and frankly shared their views on various doctrines of their churches. This was done by dialogue without any spirit of proselytism. Fellowship among theologians has resulted from these discussions and has produced much goodwill. A great harvest can be expected in the future. Dialogue itself is an achievement and an indication of a new and deeper sense of kinship than monologue could ever produce. Reuel L. Howe gives us the meaningful statement on this point when he says:

Every man is a potential adversary, even those whom we love. Only through dialogue are we saved from this enmity toward one another. Dialogue is to love, what blood is to the body. When the flow of blood stops, the body dies. When dialogue stops, love dies and the resentment and hate are born. But dialogue can restore a dead relationship. Indeed, this is the miracle of dialogue: it can bring relationship into being and it can bring into being once again a relationship that has died.[1]

The dialogue of Roman Catholic and Protestant theologians may be a beginning at the top, but it is an essential, most fruitful beginning. When resentments and hatreds are overcome, the foundation is well laid for fellowship and friendship. This is, in a sense, an ecumenical venture between Protestant and Roman Catholic theologians. We do not mean that this is a first step toward organic union between Protestants and Catholics. This was not the purpose of the dialogue, for such a union cannot be its immediate objective. But the initial communication has already created a climate in which friendship and fellowship can grow. It has also resulted in the Roman Catholic Church's greatest venture in the ecumenical field: the Second Vatican Council whose first two sessions are already matters of history.

On January 25, 1959, at the Feast of the Conversion of St. Paul the Apostle in the Basilica of St. Paul Outside The Walls, his Holiness Pope John XXIII first announced his intention to call an "ecumenical council for the universal church." The Pope stated that the primary purpose of the Second Vatican Council was the development of the Catholic faith, the revival of Christian standards of morality among the Christian people and the bringing of the church's discipline into closer accord with the

[1] Reuel L. Howe, *The Miracle of Dialogue* (Greenwich, Conn., The Seabury Press, 1963), p. 3.

needs and conditions of our times. One of the key words used
in defining the purpose of the Council was "renewal." In his
opening address to the Council the Pope further emphasized
the purpose for which the Council was being called. Said he:

In calling this vast assembly of bishops, the latest and humble
Successor of the Prince of the Apostles who is addressing you intended
to assert once again the church's magisterium which is unfailing and
perdures until the end of time: In order that this magisterium, taking
into account the errors, the requirements and the opportunities of our
time, might be presented in exceptional form to all men throughout the
world . . .[2]

The greatest concern of the ecumenical council is this: That the
sacred deposit of Christian doctrine should be guarded and taught
more efficaciously. That doctrine implies the whole of man, composed
as he is of body and soul.[3]

It is apparent that the Second Vatican Council was not called to
consider steps toward organic union with non-Roman Catholic
churches. The Fathers of the Church were summoned to study,
to evaluate, and—if need be—revamp certain aspects of the
Church's life. In the light of the growth of knowledge and the
changes of the times, the Church is summoned to a deeper
spiritual life and is called to the task of finding new springs of
inspiration, life and power that she might perform a more effective ministry among the children of men.

A call to a deeper spiritual life is a call to a closer fellowship
with Christ. Although the Pope does not state it in his message,
it seems evident that any movement of any church toward closer
fellowship with Christ will mean a closer fellowship with all
other believers who seek to draw nearer to the Lord of life. The
renewal within the Roman Catholic Church could well lead to
deeper springs of spiritual power. This renewal would be the

2 Cf. Appendix C, Pope's Address to the Second Vatican Council, p. 189.
3 *Ibid.*, p. 192.

same in quality as any that might result from that evangelism among Protestants which again highlights Jesus Christ as the central figure and power. When believers draw nearer to Jesus, they will experience a closer fellowship be they Protestants or Catholics. Drawing nearer to Jesus enables each believer to see the beam in his own eye and to be less concerned about the mote that might be in his brother's eye. A new life of dedication destroys the grounds of personal pride and humbles one to confess his own sins with sorrow and repentance.

This seems to be the point of view expressed in the testimony and writings of one young Catholic theologian. He is brave and heroic, frequently sounding like a voice in the wilderness. His voice represents not only his own opinion but reflects the attitude and thought of many leaders within the Roman Catholic Church. This young prophet, Hans Küng, professor on the faculty of Catholic Theology at the University of Tübingen, Germany, believes he speaks the sentiments of Pope John XXIII. The fact that his book received the approval of his bishop and wide acceptance within his Church is most significant. It means there must be others who think as he thinks, or at least believe that what he says should be said.

Although Professor Küng is concerned about reunion between Catholics and non-Catholics, his primary concern is the renewal within the Roman Catholic Church itself. He takes the position that the Roman Catholic Church should begin with reform and renewal from within before she attempts reunion. He advises that we draw closer to the power of Christ before we undertake any task that can be accomplished only by the power of Christ. He admits that there has been and will always be the necessity for renewal within the church itself because the church is made of human beings who are not perfect but are sinful creatures saved by grace. Says he:

The church is indeed essentially a creation of God through Jesus Christ in His Holy Spirit; her being can be conceived only in faith, as a holy mystery from above, but the church must not be seen only from above; she must not be deified, as though she did not consist of real men, of men as they really are. . . .

Renewal and reform of the church are pre-eminently necessary because the church consists, first, of human beings, and, secondly, of sinful human beings.[4]

The church, then, is often penalized by the imperfection of her members; those who lead need to be led by the Holy Spirit, and those who hear the confessions of others need constantly to pray: "Forgive us our sins."

Throughout his book the emphasis is on renewal. Believers must be self-critical, repentant, prayerful, and willing to suffer or to bear a cross. Such a venture with Christ will attract others as the deeds of service and sacrifice reflect the glory of God our Heavenly Father. Professor Küng calls for a new spiritual life within the Roman Catholic Church. Such is essential to drawing others. The uplifted Christ will draw all men unto Him. The Church must humble and dedicate herself anew to the Christ of the Cross. Professor Küng does not believe it is enough for the Roman Catholic Church to invite the separated brethren to return to the mother church. He believes the way to achieve reunion is for the Roman Catholic Church, as well as the separated brethren, to admit the errors of the past and to accept the responsibilities for serving the Master in all diligence:

We do not think of ourselves as well content and wholly self-sufficient while our brethren around us have to seek for what they need and do not have. We are thankful to be able to say, openly, that we owe many insights to Protestant theology which we should be sorry to have to do without. . . .

Four hundred years of fruitless appeals to the Protestants, and nine hundred of fruitless appeals to the Orthodox, are perhaps

[4] Hans Küng, *The Council, Reform and Reunion* (New York, Sheed & Ward, 1961), p. 3.

demonstration enough that this is no way to reach the goal. It cannot be a matter simply of the others' "returning," as though we had no responsibility for the split, as though it were not in the least up to us to go to meet them, and as though they had nothing whatever to bring with them—they, our brothers, lovers of Christ our Lord! There is altogether too much self-glorification and self-righteousness in such behavior, however much it may be accompanied by prayer. We are not merely to say "Lord, Lord" but to do the will of the Father. What is demanded of us is not a faith which waits inertly for others to return, but faith active through love, faith which goes to meet them. This is what the Pope wants.[5]

The words of Küng sound like a message from the soul of a man who has himself encountered the power that makes men new. His bold testimony is an indication of new insights and a new dynamic spirit that is moving within the framework of the Roman Catholic Church. It is significant that a young Catholic theologian writes with such dynamic power and with such far-reaching insight, but is more significant that he has been inspired by the liberal and devout spirit of his Pope.

The Pope was not unmindful of the need for a new togetherness between Roman Catholics and the non-Catholic brethren. This is why he established a special Secretariat for Promoting Christian Unity as part of the Second Vatican Council. He pointed out in the first announcement of his intention to call an Ecumenical Council for the Universal Church that it was to be "not only for the spiritual good and joy of the Christian people, but also to invite the separated communities to seek again that unity for which so many souls are longing in these days throughout the world."

On May 30, 1960, the Pope further re-emphasized this in a semi-public meeting of all the cardinals present in Rome. He said he would elect a Secretariat to help "the separated brethren to follow the work of the Council." On June 6, 1960, the Pope

[5] *Ibid.*, pp. 134-135.

appointed Augustine Cardinal Bea to be the president of the Secretariat. On June 24, 1960, Monsignor J. G. M. Willebrands was appointed the secretary. During September of 1960, the first group of members, consultants and the permanent staff were appointed. Others have been added since that time. On October 24, 1960, the new offices of the Secretariat opened at Via de Corridori 64 in Rome. The Pope referred to the Secretariat on Christian Unity "as a token of our affection and goodwill toward those who bear the name of Christians but are separated from this Apostolic See, to enable them to follow the work of the Council and to find more easily the path by which they may arrive at that unity for which Jesus Christ prayed so earnestly from His Heavenly Father."

The Secretariat has a two-fold purpose. Its immediate purpose was to accurately inform non-Catholic Christians on the work of the coming Council; to receive their wishes and suggestions relating to the Council, to weigh them, and if need be, to pass them on to other commissions. However, the Secretariat is not a mere information center. It aims to help guide the Council in those theological and pastoral matters which directly or indirectly bear on the problem of Christian unity. It is a Secretariat for Promoting Christian Unity. Its larger end is to aid non-Catholic Christians to find "that unity for which Jesus Christ prayed so ardently to His Heavenly Father." It must establish the exact situation of unity in various countries, determining what various non-Catholic Christians here and now have in common with the Roman Catholic Church in doctrine, discipline and cult and also how they differ from it. What are the desires of these different groups touching on the unity problem, and in what ways can the Catholic Church help them to true unity? These aims have been factually expressed by the Pope and the members of the Secretariat for Promoting Christian Unity. They give us a clear, positive, and concise picture of the purpose and function of this department which is one of the vital aspects of the Second Vatican Council. It is to this aspect of the Council that one must look for direct suggestions in the interest of Christian fellowship between Protestants and Roman Catholics.

Under the auspices of the Secretariat for Promoting Christian Unity, non-Catholic Observers and Guests were invited to the Second Vatican Council. It is historically significant that the Pope took this action because this is the first time in the long history of the Roman Catholic Church that this type of concern and consideration has been shown non-Catholics in a Council of this nature. It is due to the great ecumenical spirit of Pope John XXIII himself. It seems that the Observers and Guests approached the deliberations and ceremonies of the Council in the same spirit of understanding and appreciation as that which characterized the Pope's action. The Observers had not gone to Vatican City with any anticipation of modifying or changing the laws, doctrines, or policies of the Roman Catholic Church. They went as Observers and as Guests. As an Observer-Guest, I approached the Council in a deep spirit of expectancy and appreciation. I looked, and not in vain, to find wherever possible spiritual values that would tend to enrich the lives of all believers, whatever their Christian backgrounds.

14

THE SECOND VATICAN COUNCIL
(October 11, 1962)

OCTOBER 11, 1962, the opening day of the Council, began with overcast skies and even occasional showers. However, the sun soon broke through the threatening clouds as thousands of people hastened to St. Peter's Square to observe the parade of laymen, monks, priests, bishops, and cardinals moving toward the historic spot where the great Council was scheduled to convene. A crowd estimated at 150,000 watched as the procession, a dazzling display of color and pomp, went by. In the vanguard were members of the Palantine guards, wearing crimson jackets, tight white trousers, hip-length boots, and plumed helmets. They were assigned to guard the Papal throne inside the Basilica. Already inside the Basilica were Swiss guards in their Michelangelo designed uniforms of red, purple and yellow, with peaked helmets and armed with halberds. The Observers and Guests took their places on each side of the nave directly in front of the Papal throne. Prominent among the Council Fathers in white copes and miters were Yoshimatsu Noguchi, Bishop of Hiroshima; Leon-Étienne Duval, Bishop of Algiers, who spoke out against the extremist Secret Army Organization; the anti-segregationists, Archbishop Rummell of New Orleans, Cardinal Rugumbwa of Tanganyika, the only African Cardinal, and Cardinal Gracias of Bombay. In this aggregation were many of the older prelates who needed assistance as they moved from place to place. Time and age had taken its toll and some of them

158

were on their last journey. Several of these honored Fathers died within the next week.

With the great Basilica filled beyond capacity, the bells of more than four hundred churches in Rome began to ring, sending their joyous message across the hills and avenues, touching men, women and children in every section of the Eternal City. Inside the Basilica, the Sistine Chapel choir filled the vast church with the music of Ave Maris Stella (Hail, Star of the Sea). The great audience stood as Pope John and his attendants moved slowly and gracefully down the aisle of the Basilica. At an altar prepared for the purpose, the Pope paused with head bare and bowed upon his knees. The entire audience maintained moments of breathless silence as the leader of the great Roman Catholic Church paused in prayer to God as if in quest for guidance for the great assembly that had at long last convened. Thus the Second Vatican Council was opened. The Pope moved from the altar erected in the aisle to his throne where he conducted the rest of his part of the program and here he remained for more than three hours. The services and the Mass were in Latin, but the spirit and inspiration somehow broke through the Latin phrases and touched the hearts of Observers and Guests who had come to look but who tarried to worship. Some of us found ourselves in prayer to God that the Pope would have the strength to bear the burden of this exacting task as well as he carried the weight of more than eighty years. Never before in the history of the world had so great a crowd gathered at St. Peter's Basilica for so great a task.

It is strange how believers from different traditions could enter into fellowship with these leaders of the Roman Catholic Church when they could not follow the Latin even with the aid of interpreters and did not fully understand the words of the missal. Yet, through observing the symbols of the Cross we could catch the meaning of the whole service, for there stood the Cross, the symbol of the redemptive acts of our Christ. We worshiped with them because when we did not know what

they were doing, we knew why it was being done. Their method
was different from our methods. Their approach was not the
same as the Protestant approach, but from the observation of
the Cross, we knew that at the center of their program was
their concern for our Christ, our Redeemer, our Lord and
Master. Here were men of all ages joining in worship led by the
head of the Roman Catholic Church and his worthy assistants.
They were chanting canticles almost as old as the Church itself.
They were reading passages from their missal. They were observing things that had been within the tradition of the Church
for more than a thousand years. The gray walls of St. Peter's
Basilica resounded with the voices of the great leaders who
conducted the Mass. The exquisite and beautifully adorned
ceiling of St. Peter's lent its arching splendor to the sacredness
of the hour, while the massive statues carved by skilled hands
occupied their niches in the walls and gave silent testimony to
the history and significance of the Church of Rome. The varie-
gated costumes of the Church Fathers seemed to rival the
artistic designs and decorations reflected in the walls and naves
of the holy sanctuary.

Here was pageantry, drama, exquisite beauty, and a program
of worship well-planned and carefully executed not for pleasure
or for the excitement of the baser emotions of men, but to im-
press upon the hearts of all participants and those who observed, the high importance of the Christian religion and the
eternal vitality of this historic Church. Of course, their costumes
were more elaborate and maybe more expensive than the ves-
tures of Protestant leaders and worshipers. But why pause at
the observation of the external regalia, when the deeper meaning
was evident and the spirit of worship was so compelling? This
was a great event in history, and a moment when the Church
of Rome held the center of attention of the religious world as
leaders gathered to worship, think, and pray. Members of the
parishes of the world looked in wonderment and high expectation towards the Eternal City where their shepherd, their Pope

resided. History will long preserve the golden deeds of that solemn hour, and time will be most reluctant to erase it from her sacred scroll. In the memories of all who observed this opening of the Second Vatican Council, these experiences will live and linger as one of the most glorious possessions of a lifetime.

In addition to the beauty of the worship and the spirit of the occasion it seems that the aspirations of Protestants and Catholics, Jews and Gentiles, were caught up in certain elements of the opening address delivered by Pope John XXIII. There was much in this address that was directed to the Council Fathers and to the Roman Church itself. There were many theological positions, inferred and directly stated, on which the Roman Pontiff based his challenging message. Many of the doctrines were recognized as being distinct from those held by the Protestant Church. But many of the great truths expressed in this message were too universal to be restricted to any church, too basic to be claimed by any group of believers as their particular truth, and too much in harmony with the divine plan for human redemption to be catalogued among the traditions of any church, past or present, as an exclusive possession.[1]

The speech clearly sets forth the concern of the Church to address herself to the modern situation by lending her life and influence to help mankind arrive at the creative human relations to which God has called it through the message of Jesus Christ. The answers to the world's ills and the solution to the problems of human oppression, injustice, and war are best found in the message of Jesus Christ. In his reference to Christian unity the Pope points out that this is to be achieved only as those who are not in the fold of the Roman Church seek and come into the mother church. He then points out three signs of the working of the spirit of unity for which Jesus Christ prayed. First is unity among Catholics; second, the unity of prayers and desires of the separated Christians to return; third, the unity of admira-

[1] Because of the significance of the Papal address, the full text of it is given in Appendix C, p. 188.

tion for the mother church among the non-Christian religions. The interesting thing at this point is that the message is concerned about Christian unity. The way to such unity was given by the Pope in the light of the doctrine of the Roman Catholic Church. With him it could not be otherwise. But as a Protestant my greatest appreciation for this part of the message rests in the Pope's deep concern for Christian unity. Protestants differ as to the method of achieving this unity, but all must agree that the desire for said unity as expressed by the Pope is both logical and becoming the Christian spirit and the Christian purpose. The message further makes it clear that the Council was not called to make any change in any of the Church's doctrinal truths or to lay plans to negotiate with other groups separated from the Apostolic See, but rather to encourage and to inspire the separated children to return.

This position of the Pope on the matter of unity may well be the position that the Second Vatican Council will take. His reference to those not within the fold of the Roman Catholic Church was not hostile, but kind and Christian in spirit. Said he in so many words, the Church in dealing with those not in her fold should not do so with severity as in the past but with the "medicine of mercy." It was his position that the Church attracts by demonstrating the vitality of her teaching. Experience has taught that violence does not pay. The Church as the loving mother of all must show kindness to the "children" separated from her. He refers to those believers outside of the Apostolic See as separated Christians.

In this message runs a positive note of concern for Christian unity and fellowship. There is in it no element of compromise and no indication of retreat from the historic position of the Roman Catholic Church. But there is present a tender concern that reflects not only the spirit of the Pope himself but the quality of spirit that is a part of the Christian church. As one reads this message he recognizes the presence of some of the basic ideals of Christian brotherhood and the universal principles of the church of Jesus Christ. No devout believer can follow the spirit and meaning of this message and feel free to go forth persecuting others who differ with him in faith.

A brief reflection on the text of the message addressed to humanity and proposed to the Council Fathers with the approval of the Supreme Pontiff, reveals further the deep moral, spiritual, and social concern of the Roman Catholic Church. This message was adopted by a unanimous vote with little debate or discussion.[2] This message, like the other, possesses doctrines peculiar to the Roman Catholic Church but also deals with principles that may be applied by all mankind for brotherhood, world peace, and a revival of religion.

Nothing that is done by human beings is perfect. This is true not only of men in the ordinary stations of life but also of elected and appointed leaders of state and the leaders and the followers in the Christian church. We did not go to the Second Vatican Council expecting to find every segment of the work flawless. We did not go expecting to find theological positions the same as those in our own religious traditions. It is impossible to fully assess the beauty and the import of such a conclave. When all the reports are in and all the conclusions derived, years of evaluation and application will be required before the true meaning of this meeting can be more adequately grasped. Cardinal Cushing of Boston said in a speech at a dinner given by him at the North American College in Rome for the Observers and Guests of the Second Vatican Council: "It will take a thousand years to reveal the true significance of this Second Vatican Council." In this statement the Cardinal realized how much time would be needed for the seeds planted in this meeting to come to full fruition. This is a great prophecy. Its fulfillment awaits the movement of years and the testimony of centuries.

However, there are some few things that the Council has al-

2 See full text of the Message, Appendix C, p. 188.

ready achieved. It has shown how deeply concerned the Roman Catholic Church is with the task of meeting the needs of modern men and of answering the questions of present day society in language that is understandable. A new spirit of goodwill towards non-Catholic believers and a desire for the unity of the Christian church has been demonstrated. It has revealed a deep-seated longing on the part of Pope John XXIII and many of the Church Fathers for a renewal of the life of the Roman Catholic Church itself. This is another example of how the Church shares the spirit of reformation within its own fellowship. The presence of ninety per cent of the leaders of the Church, the serious approach to the task at hand of the 2,600 bishops, representing 550,000,000 believers scattered around the world, told of a vitality that is still active in spite of the perils through which the Church has passed. These leaders had not come to try rebellious persons for their sins or to excommunicate those who were found unworthy or guilty. They had not come to condemn other religions or Christian groups for their views and their separation from the Roman Church. Rather, they had come in quest of new insight and a heroic commitment to the task of helping lost men to find salvation.

How deep-seated in the hearts of both Pope John XXIII and the Church Fathers was the concern for spreading the principles of Jesus Christ throughout all the world is reflected in some of the moving events that transpired after the closing of the first session of the Second Vatican Council. These events tell us that underneath all the pageantry and beauty of the first session of the Council the Spirit of God was at work in the interest of the unity of the church and the victory of the Kingdom of God among the children of men.

A few months after the toil, rigors, and strain of the Council, Pope John XXIII committed himself to the task of completing a message to both the Church and the world in the interest of world peace. On the 11th day of April 1963, the fifth year of his pontificate, Pope John XXIII sent his now historic encyclical,

Pacem In Terris (Peace on Earth). This was the first encyclical addressed not just to the bishops and faithful of the Church but to all men of goodwill. It is a blueprint for world peace based on truth, justice, freedom, and goodwill. It gathers up the aspirations, the dreams, and desires of Protestants and Catholics, Jews and Gentiles, and on such a platform the Christian world can stand as it launches a united effort for the victory of peace in our day.

A few days after this final message to the world, about the evening of June 3, 1963, Pope John laid down the burden of his ministry and retired to eternal rest. He left to his Church, to the Christian world, and to mankind, a legacy of sacrificial service in the interest of brotherhood, goodwill, and world peace. The Church Fathers apparently recognized the spiritual legacy of their late pope and were guided in their deliberations to make choice of Pope Paul VI, who himself was committed to the continuation of the ecumenical labors of his predecessor. Under his guidance the second session of the Second Vatican Council has implemented many of the dreams and desires of the late Pope John XXIII, and there seems to be no turning back on the part of the Church Fathers from the high ideals of Christian brotherhood, Christian fellowship, Christian unity, and the urgent task of helping to implement the historic prayer of Jesus, "That They May Be One."

Whatever the future might be, no evil or vandal hands can ever snatch away the above-mentioned achievements of the past, and no iconoclast will ever thoroughly destroy the image of Pope John XXIII as a messenger of goodwill, or eradicate the constructive efforts for Christian unity that are now precious gems and living facts among both Catholics and Protestants. Such precious spiritual seeds planted in the fertile soil of this age promise a rich harvest in the years to come.

15

FROM RUDYARD TO ROME:
THE STORY OF A RELIGIOUS PILGRIMAGE
OF A PROTESTANT

FROM THE STANDPOINT of geography, Rudyard, Mississippi is a little flag-stop on the Y. & M. V. Railroad between Memphis, Tennessee and Clarksdale, Mississippi. It has one store, one gin, and about two houses. Smaller today than it was forty years ago, it is a little spot about two and a half miles from my birthplace. In my early life, it was our nearest post office and trading post. As a well-defined region, Rudyard is not known in the geography of America; yet it is not too far from Rome, Italy, by air. If one takes a train to Memphis, Tennessee, he can soon make connections by plane for Rome.

But Rudyard is more to me than a little flag-stop on a railroad. It represents, in the main, the place of my birth, childhood, and early training. Here I learned for the first time the responsibility of being a person. This came with my initiation into society and with my friendship with other members of our community. Rudyard represents the scene and the occasion of my beginning as a Christian. I was converted here as a child, accepted the Christ-way of life as the way of salvation, and for the first time, learned to rely on the love of God in Christ Jesus for salvation, for guidance, and for the hope of eternal life. The rudiments of the Christian faith were taught by humble parents, by rural district preachers, and by farmers who gave only part of their time to the work of the Christian ministry. I soon fell in love with the Bible as the Holy Book, and read it constantly and daily for light, knowledge, spiritual nurture, strength and spiritual growth. It was in these circumstances and these surroundings that I was called to preach and embraced my life's work.

Rudyard was a Baptist community; most of the large rural district churches and those in the small towns in Coahoma County were Baptists. My community represented orthodox Baptists, and I was taught and learned early to believe that the Baptists were the only true religious body. All the rest were wrong. There was a small minority who did not follow in the Bible-way and who comprised the smaller churches of our community: Methodist, Holiness or Pentecostals. Few if any of the other Protestant groups were heard of among us.

The distinguishable feature among Baptists was their form of baptism by immersion. In the early days I never heard of a Roman Catholic and did not know of any Greek Orthodox or Coptic Christians. Everybody who was not a Baptist needed salvation. There were many streams, creeks, lakes and rivers, and hence there was no legitimate excuse for anyone refusing to be baptized by immersion, for there was "much water." I learned to think that Baptists had no dealing with other religious groups or denominations. We did not go to their churches. They were not welcomed to ours, especially on Communion Day. We took great pride in the fact that unlike other denominations our name appeared in the New Testament, and we constantly quoted, "In those days came John the Baptist preaching in the wilderness of Judah." The case for the exclusiveness of the Baptist Church seemed so clear and so simple that we wondered why people were so sinful and so stupid as not to accept the fact that Baptists were a chosen people of God. We were intolerant of all other religious groups and treated them at times with open hostility. This, for me, was Rudyard.

Step by step I journeyed from Rudyard, making contact with peoples in other communities and in other groups. It was my privilege to visit conventions of the student voluntary movement when great leaders like Robert E. Spear and John R. Mott were talking about the world outreach of the Kingdom of God. I was fortunate to meet bishops of the A. M. E. Church, leaders and thinkers of the other branches of the Methodist church and to hear Presbyterians and Congregationalists talk with authority and power about the wonderful works of God.

In 1937 I visited Oxford University and the Ecumenical Council On Life And Work. Men from different Protestant groups talked about the work of religion and the mission of the Christian church. It was in that service that the Archbishop of Canterbury left Lambeth Palace in London and came to Oxford to serve the communion at St. Mary's Church. There were Anglicans, Baptists, Methodists, Presbyterians, and the whole family of the Protestant world represented. From these high moments we traveled in a body to Edinburgh University, Edinburgh, Scotland, where for about ten days we were in attendance at the Faith and Order Movement where men of different theological positions worked together freely without conflict.

My presence in 1948 when the Conference on Life and Work and the Conference on Faith and Order came together to form the World Council of Churches marked a new venture and a new discovery. When the World Council of Churches met in 1954 on the campus of Northwestern University (Evanston, Illinois), I was a part of that meeting and a participating delegate. At this time I was elected to my first term as a member of the Central Committee. In 1961 I again attended the World Council of Churches in New Delhi, India, and after this meeting paid my first visit to the Pope in Rome. These experiences taught me tolerance and led to a search into the meaning of other religious points of view and other Christian positions. These preliminary steps prepared my mind and my spirit to go to Rome.

Rome is built on seven hills and situated on both banks of the Tiber River. With a population today of two million souls, it is the capital of Italy and was for more than one thousand years the capital of the Roman Empire, the home of the Caesars, and for a period the proud mistress of the world. It was the cradle of much of western culture, the hub of law and organization as it is known in the western world. Rome is the focal point in modern history and is still filled with monuments in brick, marble, and stone that mark significant events of history and of the growth of human society. But I think of Rome as a place of great religious concern. It is the headquarters of the Roman Catholic Church which is the world's strongest single Christian group in numbers, history, organizational structure, economic possessions, and world participation. The Roman Catholic Church is the only Christian body that has an independent religious state with the civil structures similar to those found in other political states. Rome is the symbol and the name for the most authoritarian Christian group in the world. According to the official voice of the Church, it is the headquarters of the mother church. As the scene of the Second Vatican Council, Rome represents the most recent drama of the Christian struggle for world fellowship and for the unity of all believers. In spite of the rigid pattern of its theology and its ecclesiology, the Second Vatican Council saw the Roman Catholic Church make the greatest gesture in its history on behalf of a more tolerant and more friendly relationship between herself and her Protestant brothers.

For many reasons, Rome was the unique place for such a meeting of both Catholic Fathers and Orthodox and Protestant Observers and Guests. First, one sees here evidences of the long and continuous strides of the church and of Christian history. In Rome, art, science, and literature have labored, but not in vain, to preserve for posterity a record of the faith, deeds, sacrifices, and achievements of saints and Christian martyrs in ages past. In Rome stands the historic statue of Michelangelo's Moses in the Church of St. Peter in Chains. In Rome one finds in the Sistine Chapel the marvelous paintings of the Last Judgment.

In this Vatican museum one can never forget the precious and beautiful works of art by Raphael. In the Papal museum are many original documents copied by the hands of scholarly monks in the distant past.

On practically every street one sees marks of historic events and signs of the evolution of the human mind. Great is the history of Rome, and marvelous are her achievements in every branch of human knowledge and experience. But here also in Rome are the broken relics of buildings and memorials of persons and powers defeated in their efforts to block the progress of the church and to stop her victorious march down the corridors of history. The powers that were once arraigned against the church of Jesus Christ and united to destroy helpless people give silent testimony today of their error and their failure.

When the Pope opened the Second Vatican Council, there was proclaimed to the world that the desires of men were still toward the throne of God, and the mission of truth had not been frozen in the chilly winds of materialism. The call by the Pope to the Church for renewal, to believers for a closer fellowship in Christ, and to the nations of the world to turn from war to peace, is an indication of the vitality and the courage of the Christian church.

At one time, the most powerful, the most authoritarian, and the most far-reaching voice heard on the Tiber was that raised for the slaughter and destruction of other nations and peoples. And the most accepted music was the victorious shouts, patriotic songs, and loud acclaims for military leaders and heroes fresh from the exploits of war, announcing the subjugation of the weak and the helpless, and the capture and incarceration of the strong. But at the convening of the Second Vatican Council a different voice was heard, a voice proclaiming the victories of love and the sound of messengers rejoicing that at long last the way of war is seen to be a way of defeat.

While the old Tiber rolls on in its bed, the creative voices proclaiming the eternal gospel of Christ are heard, for it is now known that the ages have not stopped their speech, and time

has not killed the messengers. Even the Tiber must know something. If it does, it says nothing, but just keeps rolling along.
Unlike the dumb and voiceless Tiber, the Christian church
knows something and she does say something as she keeps
rolling along. The church now knows it is held by the un-
conquerable might of the Eternal God and its victory in the
past is a testimony of divine promotion. And in coming together
in a world fellowship, the church still says the present is secure,
while God holds the future in His hand.

It goes without saying that the ecclesiology of the Roman
Catholic Church differs from that of the Baptist Church and
other Protestant groups. But the Council was a fellowship that
had been brought together in the name of Jesus Christ. This
fellowship had manifested an interest in a united Christian
church with a deep concern for world peace and faith in the
gospel of Jesus Christ as the answer to the problems of sin and
evil. For we were impressed as Observers that for our Catholic
friends as for us, Christ is still the living dominating source,
the power and the reason for man's hope of salvation. In this
meeting, as in other ecumenical gatherings, the fact that the
church was still a living and victorious force in the world today
was impressive. Many other philosophies have come to naught,
and their leaders have lost their attraction. Not so with the man
of Galilee. His message still challenges the hearts of men in all
areas and manners of life. His message is still spreading from
shore to shore, from continent to continent and from pole to
pole. The sword today is no longer a symbol of political power.
History proclaims that the glorious day of the Caesars has
passed, and human thought and experience have outgrown the
ancient trust in weapons and armaments in their quest for the
great securities of life; war-making is no longer a worthy cause
for the growth of nations and the progress of a people. The
coming together of this great multitude of Christians was a
visible demonstration of the church to the world, saying that
the influence of the Cross of Christ is still spreading.

Those ancient enemies of Jesus who opposed Him and went

about to kill Him and who later plotted to imprison His church, did these wicked things in order "that the message of Jesus Christ should spread no further." But it has been twenty centuries now since the story of the kingdom started its humble journey of faith down the corridors of time. It has not stopped yet but still moves forward by the power of grace. Not far from St. Peter's Basilica the dark chambers of the catacombs still remain as a subterranean testimony of the victory of the Church over the legions of Caesar and as a reminder of the power of the Cross of love to meet the campaigns of the demons of hate. In the City of the Seven Hills not too far from St. Peter's historic church is the ancient site where helpless Christians were fed to hungry beasts of prey and their blood stained the earth while their bodies were crushed by the iron might of ferocious lions. But today this old Colosseum is in ruins and its broken walls are the relics of that savage life that labored to put the Christian church out of existence.

I left Rome rejoicing in the certainty of Christian victory, richer in the depth of Christian fellowship that extends across denominational lines and is sustained by faith, hope, and love. Great were the moments of inspiration, and glorious were the hours. For at Rome all had witnessed another high venture in Christian fellowship and had seen the Church of Rome march forward proclaiming the urgency for the answer to the prayer of Jesus Christ, "That They May Be One." Here the Church of Rome had done within her own ranks what the World Council of Churches as a fellowship of churches had done at Amsterdam, Evanston, and New Delhi.

Since my return from this Council I have been asked: "What influence did this Council have on your Baptist witness? What did the Baptist suffer in this encounter? What, if anything, did a Protestant from Rudyard lose on this pilgrimage to Rome? What has this world fellowship with others done to the parochial experiences of Rudyard? The answer is simple. A part of Rudyard has been modified and changed, for in this pilgrimage other saintly souls aside from those in the Baptist denomination were discovered. The voices of saints and heroes of the Cross who march under other denominational banners have been heard.

If Rudyard means only a narrow sectarian outlook on life, then I say with Thomas Wolfe, "I cannot go home again," nor should I go. But if one thinks of the basic principles of the Christian religion, then Rome deepened my faith in the kinship of all believers and in the universality of the grace of God. Rome did not destroy but strengthened Rudyard. The religious certainties of Rudyard still remain. The conviction received that Christ is the way to truth and to life is convincing still. The religion of the grace of God as the only source of human hope and world salvation is more powerful today than ever before.

It is true that Rudyard did not have monuments of brass, marble and stone, or any marks of ancient history; there were no works of art to remind us of the footprints of the makers of history and of the presence of conquering heroes of the past. But what was lacking by human hands had been done by the God of history in the face of nature and etched in the skies above. Rudyard had its wooded plains where the huge oak and gigantic elms grew. They stood as sentinels of power and as reminders that some great mind had built these huge trees without the use of saw, hammer, or nails. And this same Master had planted the forest and sown the fertility in the soil where seeds could sprout and crops could come and go. He had allowed flowing springs of water to gush forth from the hills and feed the running streams below that satisfy the thirst of men and beasts. His hand kept the balance between the freeze of winter and the thaws of spring. Because of Him, the laughing sunshine of summer has seen toiling creatures going forth to plant and to wait. The quiet fragrance of gardens and fields, the nocturnal music on wooded hills and grassy plains bespoke a beauty and harmony of the spheres that even the Psalmist could not surpass in his imagination. The glory of cerulean skies studded with millions of sparkling stars revealed a work of art greater than any that have been painted by human hands. In such a setting it is expected that one would learn to think of the work of God as revealed in nature. His beauty was in the flowers of the field and His tender care reflected in His provision for the beasts of the forest and the fowls of the air while the silent heavens declared His impeccable grandeur.

But the God of Rudyard was more than a God of nature. He was manifested to us as a God of love and mercy by the rustic people, including rural preachers, Christian parents, and devout saints. These believers told the story of Jesus Christ as a revealer of God and as the Savior of the world in their own humble way. The moral quality of the life they proclaimed has not been improved upon by theologians or philosophers. The certainty of their faith was beyond question, and the contagion of their passion for Christ was pervasive and compelling.

The experiences of reality at Rudyard have not faded in the acid test of this new age and even now the old hymns that we sang then still speak of spiritual verities that are as fresh as the dawn and as glorious as the sun. There is a solemn harmony between the travail of soul and the tearful melodies of the old spirituals that came forth as songs of promise from a people in the prison house of pain. The venture of faith that was Rudyard still lingers in the mind untarnished by years and undaunted by the winds of doubt.

My conversion to the Christian religion came in an old-fashioned revival meeting led by Elder L. F. Curry, the pastor of the church, and Elder Henry Jackson, my father. By any stretch of the imagination and any appeal to history these men could not be listed in the sacred line of the apostolic succession. The link is missing that would give them such a rank, but these humble preachers had received in some fashion the true story of Jesus Christ. Although ignorant of the fine points of theology, they were proclaimers of the gospel of the Son of God as they understood it.

God, then, must have ways of calling men to speak for Him aside from the line of apostolic succession. Some divine power had influenced these men to speak the truth of human redemption and had brought them into the sacred tradition as witnesses of Jesus Christ. For the story they told of the Christ is the same in quality, purity, and redemptive power as that which has come from Christian leaders and theologians whose academic attainments were far superior.

At Rudyard, God transcended the line of apostolic succession as He has done on other occasions, and by the golden chain of providence linked these rustic servants of God to the flaming resources of Pentecost. God is a spirit. His availability to the lost and the sinful is not determined by geography, or restricted by time or by culture. Here the author does not deny any of the great Christian doctrines of history but simply affirms that God was at Rudyard using rural district preachers and ordinary people to reconcile believers unto Himself.

The devout saints who first shared the story of the Cross with me were just as certain that Jesus was the way of life and the true Redeemer as were the bishops, priests, cardinals and world leaders in every ecumenical council that I have observed or attended. What I received at Rudyard remains today deeper, purer, stronger.

By experience I know that a man within the ranks of his own denomination can grow both to respect and to appreciate the religious values in others without in any way losing his personal faith and fervor. It is through this kind of appreciation and this kind of fellowship and understanding based on an eternal faith that the Kingdom of God will yet come.

16

MANY: BUT ONE

THERE ARE MANY DENOMINATIONS of Christians with various traditions, languages, and methods of interpretation. However, running through all of these is an inescapable oneness that seems to make all believers kin. As far apart as Protestants are from the Roman Catholic Church in their ecclesiology, there is a kinship between these bodies of Christians that cannot be negated. For all believers there is but one God, although the approaches to Him are varied and the theories about Him are expressed in unique systems of theology. Manifold are the ideas of God, but He still remains the one true God. While there are various forms of worship, there is one God, the Creator and the Father of us all. While there are many conceptions of Jesus Christ, many descriptions of His nature, and many stories of His relationship both to God and men, there is still the one undivided Christ, the Savior of all men who come to Him by faith. There are many forces of evil in league against the Kingdom of truth and righteousness, but there is only one Calvary, one fountain designed for the remedy of all uncleanliness.

There is but one family of the redeemed; some day this fellowship will rise above differences and accept the oneness that God has given us. God has given us the unity that we seek and has willed for us the kinship that we desire, and even now, all believers can live in this one fellowship in spite of the many languages, traditions and denominations that on the surface would tend to deny this oneness. The story of this book is the story of the ever present oneness among different groups of

Christians. There are in Protestant and in Roman Catholic circles longings and strivings to seize the basic fact of Christian oneness and make fellowship the major, and divisions the minor elements in thought and in life. It is this type of oneness that all should work to achieve and it can be achieved if we will follow the way of Jesus Christ.

I shall share an experience with you that may illustrate the fact of differences and our inescapable oneness.

On November 26, 1961, my wife and I took a private taxi from New Delhi, India, to Agra to visit the great Taj Mahal. In addition to being fascinated with the wonders of the Taj Mahal, the experience enroute taught the lesson that I seek to share. On the road we encountered many travelers and observed practically every mode of travel. Some were riding in modern automobiles, some rode in wagons drawn by mules or small beasts of burden. Some rode on the backs of donkeys; still others made their ways on slow-moving camels. There were also in this vanguard of travelers those who used elephants as their means of transportation. Hundreds of others traveled on foot, carrying their heavy burdens upon their backs. *But all of them were journeying on the same road.* Just as the travelers on that Indian road, we believers may be many in our modes of travel, but we are on the same road that leads from sin to salvation. We as believers have a common origin at the foot of the Cross. We also have a common destiny. Inquire of any group of believers: "Whence cometh thou, and whither goeth thou?" The answer is clear: "We are pilgrims from the fountain of grace enroute to the land of glory."

The writer of the Book of Revelations gives us a meaningful story. His vision is a fitting illustration of the oneness of the great host of believers. Here is a Christian writer who is freed from any taint of anti-semitism; in his vision he includes the Jewish people in the company of the sealed servants of God. He recognizes what is an inescapable historic fact, namely, that the Jewish people and the Christian family are vitally related. For

the best and the most universal in the Jewish religion was not
only prior in history to the Christian religion but was the source
of much of it. Note the author's words:

> And I saw another angel ascending from the east, having the seal
> of the living God: and he cried with a loud voice to the four angels,
> to whom it was given to hurt the earth and the sea, Saying, Hurt not
> the earth, neither the sea, nor the trees, till we have sealed the
> servants of our God in their foreheads.
>
> And I heard the number of them which were sealed: and there
> were sealed an hundred and forty and four thousand of all the tribes
> of the children of Israel (Revelation 7:2-4).

When our author had finished his statistical report of the sealed
servants of God among the Hebrews, he recognized that this
group did not exhaust the number of the company of the redeemed. Said he:

> After this I beheld, and, lo, a great multitude, which no man could
> number, of all nations, and kindreds, and people, and tongues, stood
> before the throne, and before the Lamb, clothed with white robes,
> and palms in their hands; And cried with a loud voice, saying,
> Salvation to our God which sitteth upon the throne, and unto the
> Lamb.
>
> And all the angels stood round about the throne, and about the
> elders and the four beasts, and fell before the throne on their faces,
> and worshipped God, Saying, Amen: Blessing, and glory, and wisdom,
> and thanksgiving, and honour, and power, and might, be unto our
> God for ever and ever, Amen.
>
> And one of the elders answered, saying unto me, What are these
> which are arrayed in white robes? and whence came they? And I
> said unto him, Sir, thou knowest. And he said to me, These are they
> which came out of great tribulation, and have washed their robes,
> and made them white in the blood of the Lamb.
>
> Therefore are they before the throne of God, and serve him day
> and night in his temple: and he that sitteth on the throne shall dwell

among them. They shall hunger no more, neither thirst any more; neither shall the sun light on them, nor any heat. For the Lamb which is in the midst of the throne shall feed them, and shall lead them unto living fountains of waters: and God shall wipe away all tears from their eyes (Revelation 7:9-17).

He saw another multitude that did not yield to the law of statistics, a multitude which no man could number. This multitude came from all nations and kindreds and peoples and tongues. Here is a latitude for believers from all Christian groups and denominations. They are not from any one clime or country, but from everywhere. The author could not tell how many, but he could tell who they were. "These are they which came out of great tribulation." They have had common sorrows, common problems, and kindred agonies and pain. This multitude had discovered one fountain in the which they washed their robes and made them pure, and that fountain was the Blood of the Lamb. This multitude bowed around the throne and all of them worshiped God. Whatever their backgrounds or their native tongues, their message was the same. They said, "blessing, and glory, and wisdom, and thanksgiving, and honor, and power, and might, be unto our God forever and ever." Not a multitude of gods, but only one God.

Theologians have labored hard and well to draw the line of distinction between different Christian groups, and by their logic they have defined the shades of differences by which believers are divided, so that one may know what he is and the reasons on the sectarian level. With these labors of the past we have no quarrel, but we now await a new school of theologians who will help us to rise above the landscape of divisions. We await theologians who will view the people of God from the highest peaks of divine enlightenment and who will tell us a new story of our togetherness, fellowship, and oneness in Christ. Let the learned and the devout teach us all to say that we are many families but one people traveling by many modes, and on but one highway, beset by many problems and moving at different rates of speed, but all moving towards one destiny. Even now while we are many, we are one.

APPENDICES

APPENDIX A

Text of the Message
Addressed to Humanity and
Proposed to the Council Fathers
With the Approval of the Supreme Pontiff

WB WISII to convey to all men and to all nations the message of salvation, love and peace which Jesus Christ, Son of the living God, brought to the world and entrusted to the Church.

It is in fact for this reason that we, the successors of the apostles, are united in prayer with Mary the Mother of Jesus, forming one single Apostolic Body whose head is the successor of Peter, are gathered here on the invitation of His Holiness Pope John XXIII.

In the course of our meetings, under the guidance of the Holy Spirit, we intend to seek the most efficacious ways of renewing ourselves, and of becoming the constantly more faithful witnesses of the gospel of Christ.

We will strive to propose to the men of our times the truth of God integral and pure, in order that they may understand it and accept it freely.

Conscious of our responsibility as pastors, we ardently wish to correspond to the demands of all those who seek God "si forte attrectent eum aut inveniant, quamvis non longe sit ab unoquoque nostrum."

Faithful therefore to the mandate of Christ who offered himself a holocaust "ut exhiberet ipse sibi Ecclesiam non habentem maculam aut rugam . . . sed ut sit sancta et immaculata (Eph. 5:27)," we will devote ourselves with all our energies, with all our thoughts towards renewing ourselves and the faithful entrusted to us, that the image of

Jesus Christ which shines in our hearts "to reflect the splendor of God (II Cor. 4:6)" may appear to all people.

We believe that the Father loved the world so much that he gave his Son to save it; and that he freed us from the slavery of sin through this same Son "reconciling all things in Him and through Him, re-establishing peace through the blood of his cross (Col. 1:20)" that we might be called and truly be his sons.

Moreover, we receive the Holy Spirit from the Father that, living the life of God, we may love God and our brothers, with whom we are united in Christ. We, therefore, who are the followers of Christ are not estranged from earthly concerns and toils. Indeed, the faith, hope and charity of Christ urges us to serve our brothers in conformity with the example of the Divine Master who "did not come to be served but to serve (Matt. 20:28)." Neither was the Church born therefore to dominate but to serve. "He gave his life for us and we must give our life for our brothers (I Jn. 3:16)."

While we hope that the Faith may shine more clearly and brightly from the work of the Council, we expect therefore a spiritual renewal which may also yield a happy impetus in favor of human welfare, that is, the findings of science, the progress of the arts and of technology, and a greater diffusion of culture.

We, united here from every nation under heaven, carry in our hearts the anxieties of all peoples entrusted to us, the anxieties of body and soul, sorrows and desires, and hopes. We turn our mind constantly toward all the anxieties afflicting men today. Our concern, therefore, is directed especially to the more humble, the more poor, the weaker, and, in keeping with the example of Christ, we feel compassion for the throngs who suffer hunger, misery and ignorance. We are constantly attentive to those who, deprived of the necessary assistance, have not yet reached a standard of living worthy of man. For this reason, in the performance of our earthly mission, we take into great account all that which pertains to the dignity of man and all that which contributes toward the real brotherhood of nations. "Caritas Christi urget nos (2 Cor. 5:14);" in fact, "qui viderit fratrem suum necessitatem habere et clauserit viscera sua ab eo, quomodo caritas Dei manet in eo (Jn. 3:17)?"

The following are the two problems of greater importance proposed to us:

In his broadcast message of September 11, 1962, His Holiness Pope John XXIII stressed two points especially. First of all, he recommended everything that favors peace among peoples. There is no man who does not detest war and who does not ardently desire peace. But this is the greatest wish of the Church who is the Mother of all. Through the voice of the Roman Pontiffs, she has never ceased to proclaim not only her love for peace, but also her resolve for peace, always ready to give herself wholeheartedly and effectively to every sincere proposal. She tends, moreover, with all her strength to unite all peoples, and to create among them a mutual esteem of sentiments and of works. Is not this our conciliar assembly—admirable for its diversity of races, nations, and tongues—is it not a testimony of a community bound by fraternal love which it bears as a visible sign. We proclaim that all men are brothers irrespeotivo of the race oi nation to which they belong.

Secondly, the Supreme Pontiff urges all to social justice. The doctrine outlined in the encyclical letter "Mater et Magistra" clearly shows how the Church is today absolutely necessary to the world, to denounce injustices and shameful inequalities, to restore the true order of goods and things so that, according to the principles of the gospel, the life of man may become more human.

We have neither the riches nor the powers of the earth, but we place our faith in the strength of the Holy Spirit, promised by Jesus Christ to His Church. Therefore we, humbly and ardently, invite all to collaborate with us to establish in the world a more ordered way of living and greater brotherhood. We invite all, not only our brothers of whom we are the pastors, but all our brothers who believe in Christ and all men of goodwill whom "God wishes to have saved and led toward the knowledge of truth (I Tim. 11:4)." It is, in fact, the divine will that the kingdom of God through the means of charity, shine even now, in a certain sense, upon earth, almost in anticipation of the eternal kingdom.

It is our ardent desire that, in this world which is still so far from the desired peace because of the threats engendered by scientific progress itself—marvelous progress—but not always intent upon the supreme law of morality, the light of the great hope in Jesus Christ our only Savior may shine.

APPENDIX B

Address of the Holy Father to the Observers of the Separated Christian Churches October 13, 1962

TODAY'S MOST WELCOME MEETING is to be simple and friendly, respectful and brief. The first word which rises up in my heart is the prayer taken from the 67th Psalm, which has a lesson for all: *Benedictus Dominus per singulos dies: Salus nostra*. Blessed be the Lord now and ever, the God who bears our burdens, and wins us the victory (Ps. 67, 20).

When in 1952, Pope Pius XII most unexpectedly asked me to become the Patriarch of Venice I told him that I did not need to reflect very long before accepting the appointment. For in the undertaking there was nothing at all of my own seeking; there was no desire in my heart of being appointed to one office or ministry rather than to another. My episcopal motto fitly provided my answer: *Oboedientia et pax*.

And so when, after thirty years in the direct service of the Holy See, I prepared myself to begin a new kind of life and found myself shepherd of the flock of Venice, which I was to tend for the next six years, I reflected and meditated upon those words of the psalm: *Portat onera nostra, Deus*, God who carries us; He carries us, what we are and what we possess; with his treasure in us and with our miseries.

This same thought was present to me when I accepted, four years ago, the succession of St. Peter and it has been so in what has followed right up to the announcement and the preparation of the Council.

In so far as it concerns my humble person, I would not like to claim any special inspiration. I content myself with the sound doctrine which teaches that everything comes from God. In this sense I have considered this idea of the Council which began on 11th October to be a heavenly inspiration. I confess to you that it was for me a day of great emotion.

On that providential and historic occasion I devoted all my attention to my immediate duty of preserving my recollection of praying and giving thanks to God. But my eye from time to time ranged over the multitude of sons and brothers and suddenly as my glance rested upon your group, on each of you personally, I drew a special comfort from your presence.

I will not say more about that at the moment but will content myself with recording the fact. *Benedictus Deus per singulos dies.* Yet, if you could read my heart, you would perhaps understand much more than words can say.

Can I ever forget the ten years passed at Sofia? Or the ten more at Istanbul and Athens? They were twenty years of happy and delightful acquaintance with persons I revere and with young people filled with generosity upon whom I looked with affection, even though my work as representative of the Holy Father in the Near East was not explicitly concerned with them.

Then again at Paris, which is one of the crossroads of the world, and was especially so immediately after the end of the last War. I had frequent meetings with Christians of many different denominations.

I cannot remember any occasion on which we were divided on principle nor that there was ever any disagreement on the plane of charity in the common work of helping those in need, which the circumstances of the time made necessary. We did not haggle, we talked together; we did not have discussions but we bore each other goodwill.

One day long ago I gave to a venerable and aged prelate of an Oriental Church, not in communion with Rome, a medal of the pontificate of Pius XI. This gesture was meant to be, and was, a simple act of friendly courtesy. Not long after, the old man on the point of closing his eyes on the things of this earth requested that when he was dead the medal of the Pope should be put on his breast. I saw it myself and the memory of it still moves me. I have mentioned this episode deliberately because in its simplicity and innocence it is like a flower of the field which the return of spring allows one to pluck and offer. May the Lord always thus accompany our steps with His grace.

Your welcome presence here and the emotion of our priestly heart (the heart of a bishop of the Church of God, as we said yesterday before the assembled Council), the emotion of my beloved fellow-workers and, I am certain of it, your own emotion too, combine to show you that there burns in my heart the intention of working and suffering to hasten the hour when for all men the prayer of Jesus at the Last Supper will have reached its fulfillment.

But the Christian virtue of patience is not out of harmony with the equally fundamental virtue of prudence.

And so I say again: *Benedictus Deus pro singulos dies.* For today let that suffice.

It is now for the Catholic Church to bend herself to her work with calmness and generosity; it is for you to observe her with renewed and friendly attention.

May the inspiration of heavenly grace which moves hearts and rewards good works be upon all of you and all that is yours.

APPENDIX C

Discourse of the Holy Father Pope John XXIII on the Occasion of the Solemn Opening of the Second Vatican Ecumenical Council October 11, 1962

MOTHER CHURCH rejoices that, by singular gift of Divine Providence, the longed-for day has finally dawned, when—under the auspices of the Virgin Mother of God, Whose maternal dignity is commemorated on this feast—the Second Vatican Ecumenical Council is being solemnly opened here beside St. Peter's Tomb.

The Ecumenical Councils in the Church

All the Councils—both the twenty Ecumenical ones and the number-less others, also important, of Provincial or Regional character—which have been held down through the years all prove clearly the vigour of the Catholic Church and are recorded as shining lights in her annals.

In calling this vast assemblage of Bishops, the latest and humble Successor of the Prince of the Apostles who is addressing you intended to assert once again the Church's Magisterium which is unfailing and perdures until the end of time: in order that this Magisterium, taking into account the errors, the requirements and the opportunities of our time, might be presented in exceptional form to all men throughout the world.

It is but natural that in opening this universal Council we should like to look to the past, and to listen to its voices, whose echo we like to hear in the memories and the merits of the oldest and less ancient Pontiffs, Our Predecessors: solemn and venerable voices, throughout the East and the West, from the fourth century to the Middle Ages, and from there to modern times, which have handed down their witness to those Councils: voices which proclaim in perennial fervour the triumph of that divine and human institution, the Church of Christ, which from Jesus takes Its name, Its grace and Its meaning.

Side by side with these motives for spiritual rejoicement, however, there has also been extended for more than nineteen centuries a cloud of sorrows and of trials. Not without reason did the ancient Simon announce to Mary, the mother of Jesus, that prophecy which has been and still is true: "Behold this child is set for the fall and the resurrection of many in Israel, and for a sign which shall be contradicted (Luke 2:34)." And Jesus Himself, when He grew up, clearly outlines the manner in which the world would have treated His person down through the succeeding centuries, with the mysterious words: "He that heareth you heareth me (*Ibidem* 10:16);" and with those others that the same evangelist relates: "He that is not with me is against me; and he that gathereth not with me scattereth (*Ibid.* 11:23)."

The great problem confronting the world, after almost two thousand years, remains unchanged. Christ is ever resplendent as the centre of history and of life, goodness, order and peace; or else they are without Him, or against Him, and deliberately against His Church, and then they give rise to confusion, to bitterness in human relations, and to constant dangers of fratricidal wars.

Ecumenical Councils, however they are assembled, are a solemn celebration of the union of Christ and His Church, and therefore they lead to the universal radiation of truth, to the proper guidance of individual, domestic and social life, to the strengthening of spiritual energies, in perennial uplift towards real and everlasting good.

The testimony of this extraordinary magisterium of the Church, in the various succeeding epochs of these twenty centuries of Christian history, stands before us collected in numerous and imposing volumes, which are a sacred patrimony of ecclesiastical archives, here in Rome and the more noted libraries of the entire world.

The Origin and Cause of the Second Vatican Ecumenical Council

As regards the initiative for the great event which gathers us here, it will suffice to repeat in historical documentation Our personal account of the first sudden springing up in Our heart and lips of the simple words "Ecumenical Council." We uttered those words in the presence of the Sacred College of Cardinals on that memorable January 25, 1959, Feast of the Conversion of St. Paul, in the Basilica dedicated to him. It was completely unexpected, like a flash of heavenly light, shedding sweetness in eyes and hearts; and at the same time it gave rise to a great fervour throughout the world in expectation of the celebration of the Council.

There have elapsed three years of laborious preparation, during which a wide and profound examination was made regarding modern conditions of faith and religious practice, and of Christian and especially Catholic vitality. These years have seemed to us a first sign, an initial gift of celestial grace.

Illuminated by the light of this Council, the Church—We confidently trust—will become greater in spiritual riches, and, gaining the strength of new energies therefrom, she will look to the future without fear. In fact, by bringing Herself up to date where required, and by the wise organization of mutual cooperation, the Church will make men, families and peoples really turn their minds to heavenly things.

And thus the holding of the Council becomes a motive for wholehearted thanksgiving to the Giver of every good gift, in order to celebrate with joyous canticles the glory of Christ our Lord, the glorious and Immortal King of ages and of peoples.

Opportuneness of Celebrating the Council

There is moreover, venerable Brothers, another subject which it is useful to propose for your consideration. Namely, in order to render Our joy more complete, We wish to narrate before this great assembly Our assessment of the happy circumstances under which the Ecumenical Council commences.

In the daily exercise of Our pastor office, We sometimes have to listen, much to Our regret, to voices of persons who, though burning with zeal, are not endowed with too much sense of discretion or measure. In these modern times they can see nothing but prevarication and ruin; they say that our era, in comparison with past eras, is getting worse; and they behave as though they had learned nothing from history, which is none-the-less the teacher of life, and as though at the time of former Councils everything was a full triumph for the Christian idea and life, and for proper religious liberty.

We feel We must disagree with those prophets of gloom, who are always forecasting disaster, as though the end of the world was at hand.

In the present order of things, Divine Providence is leading us to a new order of human relations, which, by men's own efforts and even beyond their very expectations, are directed towards the fulfillment of God's superior and inscrutable designs; and everything, even human differences, leads to the greater good of the Church.

It is easy to discern this reality if we consider with attention the world of today, so busied with politics and controversies in the economic order as not to find time to attend to solicitudes of the spiritual realm, with which the Church's Magisterium is concerned. Such a way of acting is certainly not right, and must justly be disapproved; it cannot be denied, however, that those new conditions of modern life have at least this advantage, that they have eliminated those innumerable obstacles by which at one time the sons of this world impeded the free action of the Church. In fact, it suffices to leaf even cursorily through the pages of ecclesiastical history to note clearly how the Ecumenical Councils themselves, while constituting a series of true glories for the Catholic Church, were often celebrated to the accompaniment of most serious difficulties and sufferings, because of the undue interference of civil authorities. The princes of this world, indeed sometimes in all sincerity intended thus to protect the Church; but more frequently this occurred not without spiritual damage and danger, since their interest therein was guided by the views of a selfish and perilous policy.

In this regard, We confess to you that We feel most lively sorrow over the fact that very many Bishops, so dear to Us, are noticeable here today by their absence, because they are imprisoned for their faithfulness to Christ, or impeded by other restraints; the thought of them impels us to raise most fervent prayer to God. Nevertheless, We see today, not without great hopes and to Our immense consolation, that the Church, finally freed from so many obstacles of a profane nature, such as trammeled her in the past, can, from this Vatican Basilica, as if from a second Apostolic Conacle, and through your intermediary, raise her voice resonant with majesty and greatness.

Principal Duty of the Council: The Defence and Advancement of Truth

The greatest concern of the Ecumenical Council is this: that the sacred deposit of Christian doctrine should be guarded and taught more efficaciously. That doctrine embraces the whole of man, composed as he is of body and soul, and, since he is a pilgrim on this earth, commands him to tend always towards heaven.

This demonstrates how our mortal life is to be ordered, in such a way as to fulfill our duties as citizens of earth and of heaven, and thus to attain the aim of life as established by God. That is, today all men whether taken singly or as united in society, have the duty of tending ceaselessly, during their lifetimes, towards the attainment of heavenly things; and to use only for this purpose the earthly goods, the employment of which must not prejudice their eternal happiness.

The Lord has said: "Seek ye first the kingdom of God and His justice (Matt. 6:33)." The word "first" expresses the direction in which our thoughts and energies must move; we must not, however, neglect the other words of this exhortation of Our Lord, namely: "and all these things shall be added unto you (*ibid.*)." In reality, there always have been in the Church, and are still today, those who, while seeking the practice of evangelical perfection with all their might, do not omit to make themselves useful to society; indeed, it is from their constant example of life and their charitable undertakings that all that is highest and noblest in human society takes its strength and growth.

In order, however, that this doctrine influence the numerous fields of human activity, with reference to individuals, to families and to social life, it is necessary first of all that the Church should never depart from the sacred patrimony of truth received from the Fathers; but at the same time she must ever look to the present, to new conditions and new forms of life introduced into the modern world, which have opened new avenues to the Catholic apostolate.

For this reason the Church has not been present inertly at the marvellous progress of the discoveries of human genius, and has not been backward in evaluating them rightly; but, while following these developments, she does not neglect to admonish men so that, over and above sense-perceived things, they may raise their eyes to God, the source of all wisdom and all beauty; and may never forget the most serious command: "Thou shalt adore the Lord thy God and Him only shalt thou serve (Matt. 4:10; Luke 4:8)," so that it may not happen that the fleeting fascinations of visible things should impede true progress.

The Manner in which the Sacred Doctrine is Spread

This having been established, it becomes clear how much is expected from the Council in regard to doctrine. That is, the Twenty-first Ecumenical Council, which will draw upon the efficacious and important wealth of juridical, liturgical, apostolic and administrative experiences, wishes to transmit the doctrine, pure and integral, without any attenuation or distortion, which throughout twenty centuries, notwithstanding difficulties and contrasts, has become the common patrimony of men. It is a patrimony not well-received by all, but always a rich treasure available to men of goodwill.

Our duty is not only to guard this precious treasure, as if we were concerned only with antiquity, but to dedicate ourselves with an earnest will and without fear to that work which our era demands of us, pursuing thus the path which the Church has followed for twenty centuries.

The salient point of this Council is not, therefore, a discussion of one article or another of the fundamental doctrine of the Church, which has repeatedly been taught by the Fathers and the ancient and modern theologians, and which is presumed to be well known and familiar to all.

For this a Council was not necessary. But from the renewed, a serene and tranquil adhesion to all the teaching of the Church in its entirety and preciseness, as it still resplends in the acts of the Councils of Trent and Vatican I, the Christian, Catholic and apostolic spirit of the whole world expects a step forward towards a doctrinal penetration and a formation of consciences, in faithful and perfect conformity to the authentic doctrine, which however should be studied and expounded through the methods of research and through the literary forms of modern thought. One thing is the substance of the ancient doctrine of the "Depositum Fidei," and another is the way in which it is presented: and it is this that must be taken into great consideration, with patience if necessary, everything being measured in the forms and proportions of a Magisterium which is prevalently pastoral in character.

How to Repress Errors

At the outset of the Second Vatican Council, it is evident as always that the truth of the Lord will remain forever. We see, in fact, as one age succeeds the other, that the opinions of men follow one another and exclude each other, and often errors vanish as quickly as they arise, like fog before the sun.

Ever has the Church opposed these errors; frequently She has condemned them with the greatest severity. Nowadays, however, the Spouse of Christ prefers to make use of the medicine of mercy rather than that of severity; She considers that She meets the needs of the present day by demonstrating the validity of Her teaching rather than by condemnations. Not, certainly that there is a lack of fallacious teachings, opinions and dangerous concepts to be guarded against and dissipated; but they are so evidently in contrast with the right norm of honesty, and have produced such lethal fruits, that by now it would seem that men of themselves are inclined to condemn them, particularly those ways of life and well-being based exclusively on the

comforts of life. They are ever more deeply convinced of the para-
mount dignity of the human person and of his perfectioning, as well
as the duties that that implies. Even more important, experience has
taught men that violence inflicted on others, the might of arms and
political domination, are of no help at all in finding a happy solution
to the grave problems which afflict them.

That being so, the Catholic Church, raising the torch of religious
truth by means of this Ecumenical Council, desires to show Herself
to be the loving mother of all, benign, patient, full of mercy and
goodness towards the children separated from Her. To the human
race, oppressed by so many difficulties, She says like Peter of old
to the poor man who begged alms from him: "Silver and gold have I
none, but what I have I will give thee: in the name of Jesus Christ of
Nazareth, arise and walk (Acts 3:6)." In other words, the Church
does not offer to men of today riches that pass, nor promise them a
merely earthly happiness; but She distributes to them the goods of
divine grace which, raising men to the dignity of sons of God, are
most efficacious safeguards and aids towards a more human life; She
opens the fountain of Her life-giving doctrine which allows men,
enlightened by the light of Christ, to understand well what they really
are, what is their lofty dignity and their purpose; and finally, through
Her children, She spreads everywhere the fullness of Christian charity,
than which nothing is more effective in eradicating the seeds of discord,
nothing more efficacious in promoting concord, justice, peace, and the
brotherly unity of all.

The Unity of the Christian and Human Family
Must be Promoted

The Church's solicitude to forward and defend truth derives from
the fact that, according to the plan of God, "Who wills all men to be
saved and to come to the knowledge of the truth (I Tim. 2:4)," men
without the assistance of the whole of revealed doctrine cannot reach
a complete and firm unity of minds, with which are associated true
peace and eternal salvation.

Unfortunately, the entire Christian family has not yet fully attained
to this visible unity in truth.

The Catholic Church, therefore, considers it Her duty to work actively so that there may be fulfilled the great mystery of that unity, which Jesus Christ invoked with fervent prayer from His heavenly Father on the eve of His sacrifice. She rejoices in peace, knowing well that She is intimately associated with that prayer; and then exults greatly at seeing that invocation extend its efficacy with salutary fruit even among those who are outside Her fold. Indeed, if one considers well this same unity which Christ implored for His Church, it seems to shine, as it were, with a triple ray of beneficent supernal light: namely, the unity of Catholics among themselves, which must always be kept exemplary and most firm; the unity of prayers and ardent desires with which those Christians separated from this Apostolic See, aspire to be united with us; and the unity in esteem and respect for the Catholic Church which animates those who follow non-Christian religions. In this regard, it is a source of considerable sorrow to see that the greater part of the human race—although all men who are born were redeemed by the Blood of Christ—does not yet participate in those sources of divine grace which exist in the Catholic Church. Hence the Church, Whose light illumines all, Whose strength of supernatural unity redounds to the advantage of all humanity, is rightly described in these beautiful words of St. Cyprian: "The Church, surrounded by divine light, spreads her rays over the entire earth; this light, however, is one and unique, and shines everywhere without causing any separation in the unity of the body. She extends her branches over the whole world by her fruitfulness; she sends ever farther afield her rivulets; nevertheless, the Head is always one, the origin one, for She is the one mother, abundantly fruitful; we are born of Her, are nourished by Her milk, we live of Her spirit (*De Catholicae Eccles. Unitate*, 5)."

Venerable Brothers: such is the aim of the Second Vatican Ecumenical Council, which, while bringing together the Church's best energies and striving to have men welcome more favourably the good tidings of salvation, prepares, as it were, and consolidates the path towards that unity of mankind which is required as a necessary foundation in order that the earthly city may be brought to the resemblance of that heavenly City "where truth reigns, charity is the law, and whose extent is eternity (*Cir. St. Augustine*, Epistle 138, 3)."

Conclusion

Now, "Our voice is directed to you" (II Cor. 6:11) Venerable
Brothers in the Episcopate. Behold We are gathered together in this
Vatican Basilica, upon which hinges the history of the Church; where
heaven and earth are closely joined, here near the tomb of Peter and
near so many of the tombs of Our Holy Predecessors, whose ashes in
this solemn hour seem to thrill in mystic exultation.

The Council now beginning rises in the Church like the daybreak,
a forerunner of most splendid light. It is now only dawn: and already,
at this first announcement of the rising day, how much sweetness fills
Our heart. Everything here breathes sanctity and arouses great joy.
Let us contemplate the stars, which with their brightness augment the
majesty of this temple. These stars, according to the testimony of the
Apostle John (Apoc. 1, 20), you are; and with you We see shining
around the tomb of the Prince of the Apostles, the golden candelabra,
that is, the Churches confided to you. (*Ibid.*)

We see here with you the important personalities, present in an
attitude of great respect and cordial expectation, having come together
in Rome from the five continents to represent the Nations of the world.

We might say that heaven and earth are united in the celebration of
the Council; the Saints of heaven, to protect Our work; the faithful
of the earth, continuing in prayer to the Lord; and you, seconding
the inspiration of the Holy Spirit, in order that the work of all may
correspond to the modern expectations and needs of the various
peoples of the world. This requires of you serenity of mind, brotherly
concord, moderation in proposals, dignity in discussion and wisdom
of deliberation.

God grant that your labours and your work, to which look the eyes
of all peoples and also the hopes of the entire world, may abundantly
fulfill the aspirations of all.

Almighty God! In Thee we place all our confidence, not trusting in
our own strength. Look down benignly upon these Pastors of Thy
Church. May the light of Thy supernal grace aid us in taking decisions,
and in making laws; and graciously hear the prayers which we pour
forth to Thee in unanimity of faith, of voice and of mind.

O Mary, Help of Christians, Help of Bishops, of whose love We have recently had particular proof in Thy Temple of Loretto, where We venerated the mystery of the Incarnation, dispose all things for a happy and propitious outcome and, with Thy Spouse Saint Joseph, the Holy Apostles Peter and Paul, Saint John the Bapitist and Saint John the Evangelist, intercede for us to God.

To Jesus Christ, our most amiable Redeemer, Immortal King of peoples and of times, be love, power and glory for ever and ever. Amen!

APPENDIX D

Discourse of Augustine Cardinal Bea to the Observer-Delegates October 15, 1962

My very dear Brothers in Christ,

Instead of a long listing of your titles, which I certainly do respect, please allow me to address you with these simple yet so profound words, "My brothers in Christ."

This title plunges us immediately in the profound consciousness of the incommensurable grace of Baptism, which has established bonds that are indestructible, stronger than all our divisions. Christians all over the world are daily becoming more aware of these bonds. These bonds have moved authorities to delegate you as Observers to the Council of the Roman Catholic Church. And these same bonds have prompted His Holiness Pope John XXIII to create the Secretariat for Promoting Christian Unity, in order that non-Catholic Christian Communities may follow better the work of the Council.

Now that this fraternal encounter, desired by so many baptized, has become a reality, I believe that the first and most sincere feeling of all is one of a gratitude that lets us speak with St. Paul, "Blessed be the God and Father of our Lord Jesus Christ, the merciful Father and God who gives all encouragement (II Cor. 1:3)." Indeed, it is not the work of man, of flesh and blood, but a work of the goodness, mercy and grace of our God who by the merits of our God and Saviour Jesus Christ has moved all of us through His Divine Spirit—the Spirit who dwells also in the heart of each one of us—according to St. Paul: "to prove that you are sons, God has sent out the Spirit of His Son into your hearts, crying out in us, "Abba, Father!" (Gal. 4:6). "This is the Lord's doing, and it is marvellous in our eyes (Matt. 21:42)."

True, this work is not complete. There are above all a good number of venerable Orthodox Churches of the East which are not officially represented. The fact is doubtlessly painful for both sides, for them and for us. Nevertheless, we must recognize that great efforts have been made by both sides, without completely arriving at the clearance of the large obstacles that came between. There remains for us only to pray to the Divine Head of the Church that He multiply His mercies. Meanwhile, we shall exert ourselves in preventing our relations in Christ to suffer from it and that these relations be not affected by this setback. Above all, it is necessary that our faith in the irresistible efficacy of the grace of Christ and in the work of the Holy Spirit in all the baptized be not weakened.

It is without doubt in this same spirit of prayer and confidence in the grace of God and the spirit of mutual charity and trust that we all want, during the Council, to give ourselves to this task; it is a task that ultimately has been entrusted to us by Christ Himself. I hope that you all will have found in our Secretariat, in so far as it is possible, all understanding and all fraternal help that will allow you to bear your task easily and successfully. We shall try to realize little by little what perhaps could not have been done from the beginning, because, among other reasons, this is the first time such a task has been undertaken. All the members of the Secretariat will always be most willingly at your disposal and I myself shall do the same, in every measure allowed by my work within the Council.

This is the reason why I ask you to grant us complete confidence and thus to tell us very frankly—above all, during the sessions specially organized for you by the Secretariat, everything you dislike, to share with us your positive criticisms, your suggestions and your desires. Of course, I cannot promise you to find a solution for every problem. But I do assure you that we shall be grateful to you for your confidence, that we shall try to consider everything sincerely in Christ, in order to do, as far as we are permitted, everything that can be done now and in the future.

These are the thoughts that I wanted to confide in you on the occasion of this family gathering. I believe it is for all of us a spiritual feast, a kind of "agape "in Our Lord Jesus Christ, to Whom alone be glory and praise forever and ever.

APPENDIX E

Speech of Prof. Schlink Replying on Behalf of the Observer-Delegates to Cardinal Bea's Allocution Rome, October 15, 1962

Your Eminence!

Let me express to you, on behalf of the Observers and Guests, our most sincere thanks for having received us in such a friendly way. We do not think only to the present reception, but to all assistance and help you have given each one of us since the first day, together with the collaborators of your Secretariat, especially Msgr. Willebrands. I accepted all the more willingly the task, to which I have been appointed by the Observers and Guests, to express these thanks on their behalf as I have been given the opportunity since a long time already to experience your friendliness together with my Anglican friend Canon Pawley.

Most Observers have been sent here by Churches which belong to the Ecumenical Council of Churches and the Guests too, who are here, are familiar with the Ecumenical movement. We have experienced there how churches which up to now were extraneous one to the other, began a true dialogue and open themselves to a new understanding and to a mutual exchange of spiritual gifts. The encounters with the Roman Catholic Church were up to this day confined almost only to individuals or small groups. The fact that the encounter in this Council has now an official character is felt by us as a great improvement, and we are aware of the fact that it is not at all obvious that we have been given the same *schemata* that the Fathers of the Council have received, and that Your Eminence has made possible for us to express our opinions on these *schemata*. We know that we owe His Holiness the Pope himself for this possibility—the Pope who has brought out through the initiative of his heart a new climate of open-mindedness towards the non-Roman Catholic Churches. May we ask you to tell His Holiness our respectful and sincere thanks for this, and for his kind reception at the audience on Saturday night too.

Of course all the gentlemen who are here gathered see very clearly the great and deeply rooted hindrances which divide us one from the other. We would not be separated if each one of us did not feel bound to his church by God himself and we would not serve in truth the unity in Christ if we did not take seriously this situation. Yet I would like to point out two facts which strengthen our hope for a true dialogue among all of us:

The first one is a thought which Your Eminence has repeatedly expressed in your conferences during these last two years, and which now has come out also in the papal allocutions for the opening of the Council: the revealed truth is absolutely binding for all our words and deeds. Yet on the same time a distinction must be drawn between the substance of the doctrine and the formulation in which it is wrapped up (*modus enuntiandi*). I am convinced that the separated Christianity has more substance in common than it appears at first if one looks at its different formulation.

The second fact that gives us courage is the following: Your Eminence himself is a prominent representative of Biblical scholarship and the Biblical studies have increased in a significant way in the Roman Church especially after the encyclical "Divino afflante Spiritu" has been given out. Now, as the Bible is common to all of us and as today already Biblical scholarship is no longer thinkable apart from inter-confessional collaboration among scholars, we may expect much from further development of Biblical scientific research.

Let me add, to conclude, that the prayer for the Holy Spirit with which the Council has begun, was the common prayer of all of us and that we shall follow with that prayer the course of the debates at the Council.

N.B. The original text of Cardinal Bea's speech was in French. The original text of Professor Schlink's speech was in German.

APPENDIX F

Bill Regarding the Problem of Mixed Marriages Between Protestants and Catholics October 21, 1962

His Eminence Augustine Cardinal Bea,
President of the Secretariat for Promoting
Christian Unity,
Via dei Corridori 64
Vatican City

Most Honorable Sir:

In response to your invitation to the Observers and Guests at your reception at the Columbus Hotel Monday Evening, October 15, 1962, I am sending the enclosed bill for the consideration of the members of the Council.

This bill reflects my interest in Christian unity in general and a more wholesome fellowship between Roman Catholics and Protestants in particular.

I share with Professor Hans Küng the position expressed in the following statement:

"Four hundred, nay, a thousand years of separated churches cannot be crossed at a single bound. It will need step after step." (*The Council, Reform and Reunion*—Stagbook Edition, p. 274).

It is my belief that the bill presented, if adopted, would mark a step toward the high goal of goodwill and better Christian understanding.

J. H. Jackson

This seems to be an area where better understanding, better relations and goodwill could be developed between Protestants and Catholics without need for any serious modification of dogma or doctrine. According to the famous Boston letter from the Holy Office August 8, 1949 addressed to Archbishop Cushing of Boston, U.S.A., the Pope supported the idea that non-Catholics by yearning and desire may be members of the Mother Church, without enjoying all of the benefits of grace available to the full members who are in the church by Baptism, the Creeds and the Holy Communion. Gregory Baum in his book, *That They May Be One*, is a strong advocate also of membership of Protestants in the Mother Church by desire.

Pope John XXIII in his opening address to the Second Vatican Council October 11, 1962, seemed to concur in this general idea in his reference, "To the unity of prayers and ardent desires with which those Christians separated from this Apostolic See aspire to be united with us."

Since it is the generally accepted position in the Roman Catholic Church that there is a membership by desire, is it not possible to so interpret this membership that Protestants and Catholics will be allowed to join in matrimony granting their off-spring the right to become members of the Mother Church in reality or by desire?

J. H. Jackson,
October 21, 1962

APPENDIX G

Bibliography

Books

Bates, H. N., Canon of Carlisle, *Faith And Order: Proceedings of The World Conference: Lausanne, August 3-21, 1926*, Garden City, New York, Doubleday, Doran & Company, Inc., 1928.

Baum, Gregory, O.S.A., *That They May Be One: A Study of Papal Doctrine (Leo XIII-Pius XII)*, Westminster, Maryland, The Newman Press, 1958.

Birney, James C., *The American Churches: The Bulwark of American Slavery*, Third American Edition, New York, Parker Pillsbury, 1885.

Dimont, Max I., *Jews, God And History: A Modern Interpretation Of A Four Thousand Year Story*, New York, Simon & Schuster, 1962.

Dumont, C. J., O.P., *Approaches To Christian Unity*, London, Darton, Longman & Todd, 1959.

Hodgson, Leonard, *Convictions: A Selection From The Responses Of The Churches To The Report Of The World Conference Of Faith And Order, Held at Lausanne in 1927*, New York, Macmillan Company, 1934.

Howe, Reuel, L., *The Miracle of Dialogue*, Greenwich, Connecticut, The Seabury Press, 1963.

Küng, Hans, *The Council, Reform and Reunion*, New York, Sheed & Ward, 1961.

Meland, Bernard E., *The Realities Of Faith: The Revolution In Culture Forms*, New York, Oxford University Press, 1962.

Niebuhr, Reinhold, *The Nature And Destiny Of Man*, Volume I, New York, Charles Scribners Sons, 1941.

Rittelmeyer, Friedrich, *Behold The Man*, New York, The Macmillan Company, 1929.

Sheed, F. J., *A Map of Life*, New York, Sheed & Ward, 1933.

Sweet, William Warren, *The Story Of Religion In America*, New York, Harper & Brothers, 1930.

Watkins, E. I., *The Church In Council*, New York, Sheed & Ward, 1960.

Zabriskie, Alexander C., *Bishop Brent: Crusader For Christian Unity*, Philadelphia, Westminster Press, 1948.

Magazine Articles

"Council Of Renewal," *Time*, LXXX (October 5, 1962), pp. 80-86.

Fey, Harold E., "From Renewal To Unity," *The Christian Century*, LXXIX (October 31, 1962), pp. 1314-1315.

————, "Splendor In St. Peter's," *The Christian Century*, XXIX October 24, 1962), pp. 1282-1283.

Mathews, Shailer, "Doctrines As Social Patterns," *The Journal of Religion*, X (January, 1930), pp. 1-15.

"The Second Vatican Council," *The Christian Century*, XXIX (October 17, 1962), pp. 1247-1248.

"The Third Assembly Of The World Council of Churches," *The Philippine Christian*, XIII (November, 1961), p. 3.

Vischer, Lukas, "The World Council of Churches And The Vatican Council," *The Ecumenical Review*, XIV (April, 1962), pp. 281-295.

Reports

Bosc, Jean *et al.*, eds., *The Catholic Protestant Dialogue*, Baltimore, Helicon Press, 1960.

Callahan, Daniel J. *et al.*, eds., *Christianity Divided: Protestant and Roman Catholic Theological Issues*, New York, Sheed & Ward, 1961.

"Man's Dis-Order And God's Design," *The Amsterdam Assembly Series*, I, New York, Harper & Brothers, 1958.

Rouse, Ruth *et al.*, eds., *History Of The Ecumenical Movement*, Philadelphia, Westminster Press, 1954.

Six Ecumenical Surveys: Preparatory Material For The Second Assembly Of The World Council of Churches, Northwestern University, Evanston, Illinois, U.S.A., 1954, New York: Harper & Brothers.

The First Six Years: 1948-1954. A Report of the Central Committee Of The World Council of Churches On The Activities Of The Departments And Secretariats Of The Council, Geneva, Switzerland, World Council of Churches.

Visser 't Hooft, W. A., ed., *The New Delhi Report: The Third Assembly Of The World Council of Churches*, New York, Associated Press, 1962.

INDEX